6/14/98

Ha

George.

Scott, Mary, + Alex
Paul

Tips and Traps
When
Negotiating
Real Estate

Other McGraw-Hill Books by Robert Irwin

Tips and Traps When Negotiating Real Estate

Robert Irwin

McGraw-Hill, Inc.

New York   San Francisco   Washington, D.C.   Auckland   Bogotá
Caracas   Lisbon   London   Madrid   Mexico City   Milan
Montreal   New Delhi   San Juan   Singapore
Sydney   Tokyo   Toronto

Library of Congress Cataloging-in-Publication Data

Irwin, Robert.
    Tips and traps when negotiating real estate / Robert Irwin.
       p.   cm.
    Includes index.
    ISBN 0-07-032747-5
    1. Real estate business.   2. House buying.   3. House selling.
4. Mortgage loans.   5. Real estate investment.   6. Negotiation in
business.   I. Title.
HD1379.I673   1995
333.33—dc20   95-11854
                                            CIP

3 4 5 6 7 8 9 0   DOC/DOC   9 0 0 9 8 7 6

ISBN 0-07-032747-5

The sponsoring editor for this book was James H. Bessent, Jr., the editing supervisor was Jim Halston, and the production supervisor was Suzanne W. B. Rapcavage. This book was set in Palatino by Estelita F. Green of McGraw-Hill's Professional Book Group composition unit.

Printed and bound by R. R. Donnelley & Sons Company.

McGraw-Hill books are available at special quantity discounts to use as premiums and sales promotions, or for use in corporate training programs. For more information, please write to the Director of Special Sales, McGraw-Hill, Inc., 11 West 19th Street, New York, NY 10011. Or contact your local bookstore.

Contents

Preface

Negotiating is a part of living. We do it all the time. When you walk down a crowded street you "negotiate" the path you take. A couple negotiates their relationship before and during marriage, although they may not realize that's what's happening. (You take out the garbage, I do the dishes—sound familiar?) When you hire someone to work for you, whether it's cleaning your house or doing your taxes, you negotiate price and terms. Negotiation is a large part of buying an automobile. But nowhere is negotiating more out in the open or more important than in real estate.

This came home to me 37 years ago when I got my first real estate salesman's license. My father, who had been a broker for more than 20 years at that time, pointed out that although I now had the license, it didn't mean I could sell. "Selling real estate," he said, "doesn't just mean showing property or asking for listings. It means helping people get what they want." I now realize he meant, negotiating.

Over the years I've observed that a few buyers and sellers are quite adroit at getting good, sometimes terrific deals. Most others, however, simply get what the other party is willing to easily give. The difference? The first group knows how to negotiate.

Where do people learn to successfully negotiate? Are there schools that teach it?

Not as far as I know. Usually those who successfully negotiate in real estate either pick it up by doing lots of deals (experience, in other words) or just have a natural talent for it. Maybe you're gifted in this way and already know how to negotiate. But if not and if you would like to negotiate a much better deal on the next (or first) house you buy or sell, whether working with an agent or going direct, this book is meant for you.

Here you'll find the "rules for negotiating real estate." (If you don't know the rules, how can you win the game?) They are explicitly stated in the first four chapters of this book. The remainder of the book applies them to various situations such as negotiating price or commission.

These rules are simple to understand and are quickly learned. Use them correctly and I guarantee you'll get better deals, you'll buy or sell property for bigger profits, and you'll get what you truly want.

When you become a good negotiator, there's almost nothing you can't acquire.

1
The Rules of Negotiating Real Estate

Can you negotiate anything in real estate?

The answer is "Yes!" Anything can be negotiated. However, that doesn't necessarily mean that you're always going to get everything you want.

Let's say that a seller wants $120,000 for a home. You want to pay $100,000. Can you successfully negotiate the price down? Probably, depending on the seller's situation.

On the other hand, let's say that instead you want to pay $50,000 for that $120,000-priced house. Can you negotiate the price down by $70,000? Most unlikely, probably impossible, although you still might be able to negotiate a much lower price than the seller is asking.

The point here is that *negotiation* is not a magic word that will always get you everything you want. But if you use it correctly, it will get you the very best deal that can be made, every time.

How to Negotiate

In order to negotiate successfully you have to know the rules of the game. Yes, negotiating in real estate has rules. After all, baseball has rules, debate has rules, some say there are even rules for lovemaking. Why shouldn't negotiating in real estate be the same?

Here are the rules that I've found are essential, if you're going to come out a winner in every real estate deal you're in.

The Four Areas Where Negotiating Rules Apply

There are only four areas within which real estate negotiations can be held. They are:

- PEOPLE (How to handle those with whom you deal)
- TACTICS (Maneuvers that gain an advantage)
- STRATEGY (Having one)
- TIME (Getting it on your side)

In this chapter we're going to work exclusively on rules for dealing with people. In subsequent chapters we'll cover the remaining three areas.

Tip

Remember People, Tactics, Strategy, and Time. They are involved in every real estate negotiation.

Trap

If you don't know the rules of the game and the other side does, how can you hope to win?

How Good Are You at Working with People?

You will always be working with people. Deals don't exist in a vacuum; deals are about people. But how you handle the people with whom you deal often determines how successful you are at negotiating. I believe that the people part of any deal is the most important and the first rule is the most important of all.

Rules for Working with People

RULE 1—Never Offend the Buyer/Seller

RULE 2—Beware of Choosing a "Nice" Agent to Represent You

RULE 3—Never Believe Anyone Else Is Entirely on Your Side

RULE 4—Always Strive for the High Moral Ground

RULE 1—Never Offend the Buyer/Seller

It's often been said that in real estate the three most important factors in determining price are "Location, location, location!" When you are negotiating, the single most important factor in getting the deal you want is "Never make it personal!"

I've seen this rule violated more times than I want to remember. Typically it occurs in a purchase. A buyer wants a home and offers what she thinks is a reasonable price. The seller, however, figures it's worth a lot more and is offended by the offer, so he turns it down and counters at only slightly less than the asking price. Now the buyer is in a huff by the intransigent seller. As long as buyer and seller do not personally meet, but negotiations are carried out through a broker (something I do not always recommend, as we'll see shortly), progress on the deal can continue.

But just let the typical buyer and seller meet for 5 minutes and the deal is history. The buyer will quickly tell the seller how ridiculous the counteroffer is. The seller will tell the buyer that she can't recognize true value. The buyer may counter with a comment about the seller's deficient intelligence. The seller may make a disparaging remark about the buyer's forebears.

Very quickly negotiations break down into dispute. Both sides take it personal and neither wants to deal with the other "no matter what the price!"

Of course, in the real world no one is going to refuse to buy or sell "no matter what the price." But if the buyer offends the seller (or vice versa), the price could end up being a lot worse for the offending party.

Tip

When you're negotiating, think of it as business. Yes, occasionally you may want to appear injured or aggrieved by something the other party says or does, but only as a ploy. Never take it personally and, if you're smart, never do anything to let the other side take it personally.

The wisdom of never offending the other party came home to me once again only a short while ago. A close friend was involved in a quarrel over a purchase. My friend had bought a lot in the mountains and began construction on a home. During excavation for the foundation, she discovered that an old, large, unused diesel storage tank was buried there. It had been used to store fuel for logging equipment. The contractors began removing the tank only to discover it still contained some fuel and was leaking. The ground surrounding it was soaked in diesel fuel. The building inspector noticed this and eventually the county environmentalist required that hundreds of yards of contaminated soil be hauled 350 miles away to a toxic waste dump site. The cost was more than $10,000 and my friend, naturally, wanted the seller to pay for it.

The seller "stonewalled," claiming that he had disclosed the problem and that my buyer friend had understood and had agreed to shoulder all the cost of removal. That, in fact, was the reason he had sold for what he claimed was such a low price.

According to my friend, this was simply untrue and she had every right to be offended. Her legal recourse was to get an attorney and sue. At the very least the seller would have had to pay some of the cost, very likely all of it.

But my friend really didn't want to expend the time, emotional stress, and cost of litigation (something more people should consider before going to court). So she negotiated instead. She met with the seller and she did indeed bring her attorney, who in no uncertain terms explained what he could and fully intended to do to the seller.

However, my friend was cordial, never mentioned the obvious (that the seller had outright lied and was continuing to lie), chatted in a friendly matter, and made it perfectly clear that she didn't consider this a personal matter. It was strictly business.

The next day the seller called my buyer friend on the phone and asked if there wasn't some way they could compromise. She replied that it was nice of him to call, but she really didn't see how a compromise was possible. He had put the tank in. Between the two of them, they knew she hadn't known about it. However, if he wanted to pay for removal costs, she would certainly not add on any of the hefty legal charges that were sure to be involved in a lawsuit. He said he would think it over.

Two days later he called back and said that because she was such "a nice gal," he'd take care of it.

Yes, it's obvious he was wrong, she was right, and it ended the way it should. But consider what the outcome could have been if my friend had taken it personally, accused the seller of lying, refused to talk to him, or even attacked him personally. He may have felt cornered and forced to hire his own attorney to defend himself. The outcome might have been the same, but it could have taken years, cost tens of thousands of dollars for both of them, and kept my friend from getting on with her life.

Trap

Beware of taking your frustrations out on the other party. You may just supply the ammunition that party needs to shoot you down.

Think about it. Would you rather deal with someone whom you find pleasant and likable or with someone whose guts you hate? Would you prefer to pick up the phone and call a person who you know will respond warmly, or someone who will start yelling at you? Years ago I had a boundary dispute with a landowner and called him to ask if we couldn't find a way to work together and settle it. He harangued me on the phone, accused me of trying to high-pressure him (which I was not doing), called me a liar and a cheat, and finished by telling me he'd "see me in court." Now, was I going to call him back and attempt to work out an amicable settlement? Or was I going to wash my hands of it and turn it over to my attorney to handle? In the end, I did prevail. But it took longer and cost more. To this day we don't speak, though we own property next door to each other.

RULE 2—Beware of Choosing a "Nice" Agent to Represent You

This is a simple rule to understand, but difficult to follow. Most of us really don't want a lot of hassle in our lives. Therefore, when it comes time to find a real estate agent, we often choose the "nicest" one. That usually means the agent who is pleasant, offers the least amount of resistance, goes along with what we say, and generally makes us feel good.

But that's not necessarily the best agent to have. For example, when selling a property, the agent has a duty to inform us of the true market price of the property, as best as it can be calculated. But we often don't like to hear that our property is worth less than we think it is. So the "nice" agent may just agree with whatever price we have in mind, hoping that later on when it doesn't sell, we'll come down. We would be better off with a hard-nosed agent who would say, "You may want $130,000, but it's worth only $115,000." That's not a nice thing to hear. But if it's the truth, it may mean the difference between selling or waiting a year and not being able to dump the property.

On the other hand, there are buyers who fall in love with the occasional agent who takes them all around showing them wonderful properties, most of which they can't afford. Or occasionally an agent who doesn't inform us that the offer we are making is unrealistically low. Or, once in awhile in the worst case, an agent is so nice that he writes up our offer with the price and all the conditions we want. Then, when the sellers reject it out of hand, he brings back a counteroffer with the price and conditions the sellers want, never making any effort to be realistic with either party. The result, almost always, is no deal. The agent is simply too "nice" to be a good negotiator.

Tip

I want an agent who represents me to be hard-nosed, irritating, and determined—someone who learned his or her business in the backrooms and who tells it like it is and gets what he or she goes after. I want the other guy to have the "nice" agent.

RULE 3—Never Believe Anyone Else Is Entirely on Your Side

Trust in yourself. You're the only person in the world who has your own interests totally at heart.

If you're a buyer, would you go up to a seller, show your bank accounts, explain how desperate you are to buy the property, and then ask the seller to tell you what to offer?

If you're a seller, would you tell a potential buyer your absolute bottom line and then ask that buyer to make you a better offer?

No sane person would do such things. Yet, every day real estate buyers and sellers allow others to make decisions for them. Those others could be an accountant, a relative or friend, or even a real estate agent. Yes, you certainly want to ask others for advice. And the point here is not that these people will consciously deceive or purposely lead you astray when you ask. It's just that everyone's interests, of necessity, are different. Each of us has our own goals and yours are always going to be different, and sometimes conflict with, mine.

Let's consider an agent, who is presumably acting in your best interest. (An agent usually has a fiduciary responsibility to look out for you—see Appendix 2 for more on an agent's responsibilities.) While an agent may indeed want to get the best buy in a house for you at the lowest price, or to sell your current home for the highest amount, that agent also needs to make deals on a regular basis in order to survive.

A good agent will always strive to put his or her client's interests first. Yet, even the best agent may occasionally suggest that you, as a buyer, make a higher offer than you want or that you, as a seller, accept a lower offer than you want, rationalizing that it's in your best interest because it will mean you'll get (or sell) a property. Of course, how can the agent completely put out of his or her mind that a sale will also mean a commission for him or her?

Tip

In business, and to a great extent in life, a little bit of skepticism is a good thing. If you take everything with a small grain of salt, you'll find that not only are your meals tastier, but your real estate deals are sounder.

RULE 4—Always Strive for the High Moral Ground

This may seem a peculiar rule, since, after all, you're presumably not trying to do anything dishonest or illegal. However, there are more ways to kill a deal than being dishonest or illegal. If you portray yourself as tricky, underhanded, or sneaky, you are sure to undermine the other side's confidence in you and once that's eroded, successful negotiating will become increasingly difficult.

For example, I once had a buyer (I represented the seller) who presented an earnest money check for $2500. I noticed that he had written out fifteen hundred while using the numbers "2500." For all practical purposes the check was uncashable and useless. Of course, it could have simply been an accident in drawing out the check, which is what he claimed and eventually wrote out a new and correct draft. However, my seller was put on guard and thereafter saw the buyer as sneaky and untrustworthy. Negotiations became awkward because from that point on, the seller trusted nothing the buyer said or did. Eventually, the sale fell through—I believe, simply because the buyer tried to pull a fast one on the deposit check.

In another instance the seller described the property as being in perfect condition with no faults or problems. But an inspection revealed a drainage problem that caused the basement area to flood each winter. There was no way the seller could not have known about this, and from that time forth the buyer was suspicious about everything in the house, demanded a second inspection, and challenged all sorts of things from the roof not leaking to there being improper wiring. Eventually the deal was made, but only after extended negotiations, written inspection reports, and concessions on the part of the seller with regard to price and financing. All this could have been avoided if the seller had simply come clean right at the beginning.

Tip

Successful negotiations are built on trust. Anything you do to limit or destroy that trust will harm those negotiations.

This point has some subtler ramifications as well. Let's say that there is some matter over which you refuse to compromise. Maybe the buyer wants you to rebuild a wall at the back of the property, a wall that is currently leaning over and looking as if it might fall. You don't want to rebuild and you simply say no.

Now the buyer begins thinking to herself, "Why doesn't he want to do that? Is it just the money? Or is there something about that wall that he's not revealing? Maybe the ground out there is bad. Maybe there's a problem with the neighbor. Maybe...."

An arbitrary refusal to yield on your part can be interpreted as an ethical problem—you have something to hide. On the other hand, if you refuse to yield, but provide an explanation that seems somewhat reasonable, your motives are no longer suspect. For example, you explain that you had the wall fixed just 2 years ago. You paid a lot of money and the workers simply did a bad job. As a matter of principle, you simply will not pay for it again.

"Okay," the buyer may think. "You're not too smart when it comes to hiring a wall contractor. You're stubborn about taking a loss. I can live with that, as long as you're not trying to cheat me!" Your explanation makes it rational and understandable. You're still operating on a high moral ground.

Tip

Never do anything that will make you look like a sneaky person. Always portray yourself as taking the moral high ground.

You are making a legitimate offer with a legitimate deposit check. You are willing to make any legitimate compromise. It makes you look reasonable and trustworthy. It gives your opponents the hope that you're someone they can, and will want to, deal with.

Trap

It's almost impossible to make a deal with someone who is, or at least appears to be, untrustworthy. If the other side is so distrustful that the only way he or she will deal is through a lawyer, you can probably kiss the sale good-bye. Most deals are made on a handshake (trust) with the paperwork to follow.

2
Tactics That Win

Do you fold when your opponents unleash a psychological attack at you? You have to know how to disarm it. On the other hand, you may want to play psychological warfare yourself. (See Rules 12 and 13.)

The following rules aren't presented so that you can gain an unfair advantage. Rather, it's vital that you be aware of them so that you're on a level playing field. These are essential rules that you need to know in order to negotiate successfully. You need to recognize when the other side uses them, and you need to able to use them yourself when necessary.

- PEOPLE (How to handle those with whom you deal)
- **TACTICS (Maneuvers that gain an advantage)**
- STRATEGY (Having one)
- TIME (Getting it on your side)

Rules for Tactics That Win

RULE 5—Disarm a Psychological Attack by Drawing Attention to It

RULE 6—Be Irrational, Occasionally

RULE 7—Strive to Be Innocent

RULE 8—Always Ask "Why?"

RULE 9—Question Authority

RULE 10—Challenge the Written Word

RULE 11—Listen Carefully

RULE 5—Disarm a Psychological Attack by Drawing Attention to It

Thus far we've been discussing strategies that will help you get what you want in negotiating. In essence, we've been fighting fair. Everything is aboveboard and out in the open.

However, sometimes you'll get into a negotiation that's dirty. The other side may not play by the rules of good conduct. The other side may resort to psychological warfare.

You're a woman and you're presenting an offer to buy a property to a male seller. He is very nice to you. He pulls out the chair for you to sit down. He asks if you'd like some coffee or other refreshment. It's nice, but a bit irritating. There are two agents present and he begins addressing them and ignoring you, even though you're the principal, the buyer. You hear remarks such as "She probably can't understand this, so let's see if we can make it simpler." Or "Let the lady talk before we get on with things." Or after you make a comment, "She's sweet, isn't she?"

Yes, the remarks are obviously sexist. But more important to the deal, they are condescending. Their real intent is to neutralize you as a force, a power in the negotiations. They aim to reduce the value of your opinions and arguments. If you let them continue, you won't be able to participate as an equal member and will ultimately get a much lesser deal.

This is a psychological attack on you. The way to counter it is to bring it out in the open. You might say something such as "I can't help but notice that many of your remarks are disparaging toward my sex. If you're hoping to get a better deal by belittling me, I'm afraid you're wasting your time. I'm the buyer and you have to deal directly with me." I don't think you'll hear many more condescending remarks.

Or let's say you're a seller whose property has gone up in value enormously since you bought it 20 years ago (just by chance the area turned into one of the most desirable neighborhoods in the state). You paid $25,000. Today, it's selling for $470,000. That's a lot of money to you, since your income has never been over $35,000 a year.

You're starting to negotiate with the buyer's agent who smiles at you and says, "It's amazing isn't it. You're going to get nearly half a million dollars for your property. Isn't it wonderful?"

Of course it's wonderful, you smile back. Then the agent continues, "I know you don't know about big money. This is sort of out of your league, isn't it? Why don't you sit back and let me handle things?"

Again, this is a psychological attack. If it happens once, you can ignore it and just figure that the other party is a jerk. If it continues to occur and begins to affect your ability to negotiate, you can end the attack by bringing attention to it.

"You seem to be suggesting that because this deal involves a large sum of money, I'm somehow less capable. I consider this a rather obvious attempt to gain a psychological advantage. I assure you I am not going to settle for less just because of the amounts involved." Having said that, there's every chance you will get every penny you deserve.

Psychological attacks usually are intended to belittle you in one way or another. As we've seen, they might be aimed at your sex or background. They could just as easily be targeted at your intelligence or your experience. For example, as a buyer you insist on presenting your own offer. You sit down to negotiate and the seller's agent immediately asks, "Are you a real estate broker?"

"No," you reply truthfully.

"Are you at least a real estate salesperson?"

Again, "No."

You hear a "Humph." You shrug and begin presenting your offer. As you are doing so you hear, "Someone who had experience in real estate would never make an offer like this." Later, "The terminology is all wrong; we'll have to rewrite it." Then, perhaps a little more directly, "Wouldn't you feel more comfortable having an agent or someone who knows the ropes present this?"

Please keep in mind that it doesn't matter whether your offer is good or bad or whether you know what you're doing or not.

You are being psychologically attacked at the level of your experience and knowledge. The other party isn't saying, "I don't like your offer," or "I want to negotiate some of the terms or the price." The seller's agent is saying, "You're too naive or too stupid to be in this game." The attack is personal and if you let it continue, you may soon feel embarrassed and may find yourself accepting terms and conditions and a price that you don't want.

Again, the way to disarm this attack is to bring it out in the open. "Am I hearing correctly? Are you saying that I'm too ignorant to make an offer on your property? I'm the first to acknowledge that I don't 'know it all,' but I'm ready and able to learn. If there's a problem with my offer, something that you don't understand or that you find is presented in an unclear manner, tell me what it is and I'll explain it further. In the future, however, I suggest we stick with the issues and avoid personal attacks."

Trap

If you allow the other party to continue a psychological attack unhindered, he or she may press it to the point where you will lose in a deal.

Tip

As soon as you unveil a psychological attack for what it is, its power vanishes and the other side will be forced to stop using it.

The real trick, of course, is to avoid succumbing to the psychological attack. If you believe that you are weaker because of your sex or that you don't know how to handle "serious money" or that you're stupid or ignorant, then you lose automatically. On the other hand, if you've a bit of self-confidence and recognize the attack for what it is—nothing more than a weapon (albeit a dirty one) in negotiations—you can neutralize it by bringing it out into the open.

I've had some small experience with computers and am occasionally called upon to help teach people the rudiments of how to use them. Very often these people are totally computer illiterate and worse, having never worked with a computer, are highly intimidated by it.

I have learned that the first thing I must do is get rid of their intimidation: otherwise, they'll never learn anything about computers. So I always tell them, "If you think you can't learn to use a computer, you never will. On the other hand, if you believe you can learn to use one, I can have you up and running in 30 minutes."

In real estate negotiation, the argument would go something like this: "If you believe the psychological attack the other party makes, you'll never get the deal you want. But if you believe that it's just a weapon used by the other side and disarm it by bringing it to everyone's attention, you've got a good chance of getting everything you want."

RULE 6—Be Irrational, Occasionally

Tip

If the seller thinks you're a little bit crazy, he may be more inclined to accept a goofy offer. After all, what can you expect from someone who's nuts?

This doesn't mean you should be carrying on conversations with spirits or foaming at the mouth. Rather, it means that you always want to keep the other side guessing about what you will and won't do, and one of the best approaches is to make people think you're a little bit *irrational*. (The word, after all, suggests that you take actions that to others appear to be against your own advantage. In truth, it really means that others simply don't understand your "rationale.") There's nothing to help keep your morale higher than to know you have the other side off balance.

The best application of this rule that I ever saw had nothing to do with real estate, but instead with the world of politics. President Richard Nixon always sought to keep his opponents off balance by convincing them that he was just a tiny bit crazy. Push him too far, and who knows what could happen? As President he might launch nuclear missiles...or send troops into Cambodia...or reconcile differences with China. He even said as much.

While it remains for history to ultimately judge his actions, to me it seems clear that Nixon, in truth, may have been many things, but was anything but irrational. I can still remember his fall from popularity during the scandal over the break-in at the Democratic headquarters in the Watergate building. Nixon was vilified, and congressional hearings were held minutely investigating every aspect of his presidency, including audiotapes of conversations. He was put under a microscopic examination that very few of us could have emotionally survived. Newspaper and television pundits repeatedly wondered about his grasp on reality and his ability to handle presidential issues, given the stress of the situation. People feared the "irrationality factor."

And that gave him an edge. Nobody wanted to push him too far. In my opinion it allowed him to hang on for far longer than he might otherwise been able to.

Yet, from his perspective, it seems to me he acted with great rationality through it all. While under fire, he continued to fulfill the basic functions of his office, as best he could, given the circumstances. Only when it became perfectly clear that he had completely lost the support of his own party, did he choose to resign. And he did that with remarkable grace.

The man was certainly calculating. But I seriously doubt if anything he ever did could be considered truly irrational.

Something similar (in terms of "acting" irrational) was the case with a friend of mine who bought and sold an enormous amount of investment real estate, making quite a bit of profit along the way. Jerry negotiated his own deals with buyers or sellers, although I occasionally sat in as an agent. Often, just when things were the most serious in the negotiations, he would surreptitiously wink at me and then all hell would break loose. Once I had trouble concealing a smile when in the middle of a serious discussion about price, Jerry asked a seller if he would accept a truckload of potatoes to sweeten the deal.

The poor seller didn't know if my friend was making a real offer, or was just plain crazy. And Jerry didn't help him out. He began extolling the virtues of baked and fried potatoes, even potato skins. He said he could have the shipment delivered and dumped at the seller's back door.

"I don't want potatoes," the seller said in frustration. "I just want to work this deal."

"It's potatoes or nothing," Jerry replied and went into the kitchen for a cup of coffee.

The seller leaned over and asked me if Jerry had a problem. I replied that he was a serious buyer making a serious offer, although he himself was a bit eccentric. The seller nodded in agreement. Later that evening the seller accepted Jerry's offer almost in total.

Why would irrationality help Jerry? When my friend pulled one of his calculated "irrationality" stunts, more often than not the routine broke the carefully built-up understanding the other party had of my friend. One moment the other person, buyer or seller, thought he or she had a handle on what Jerry really wanted out of the deal and how far he could be bent. The next moment the other party was thrown into confusion, concluding that he or she had no idea what Jerry's bottom line really was.

Of course, it doesn't always work that well. Sometimes, when you're dealing with a really solid adversary, it doesn't work at all. But, as with other devices, it can cause a "change-up" which acts to keep your opponent off balance.

RULE 7—Strive to Be Innocent

Have you ever noticed that as soon as people admit they really don't understand something, a lot of other people rush in to help them out? Try it with a group of friends. The subject doesn't really matter, but wait until real estate comes up and then say something like, "I hate to admit it, but a lease/option is over my head. What exactly is it?"

You've just given every person around you who knows (or thinks he or she knows) what a lease/option is the opportunity to shine. They can suddenly show off their knowledge and be a "good guy" by helping you out at the same time. It's hard to turn down such an appealing role. Of course, now you listen and learn what they know—and don't know. Appearing innocent is a great way to learn a lot.

Chet, another real estate friend of mine, is both a broker and an investor. When it comes time to negotiate, he kind of turns the toe of one foot inward, looks a little shy, and in his best country-boy fashion says something like "Shucks, I'm just the new guy, here. You people are all the experts, so you're going to have to help me out understanding this deal."

The others usually smile to one another thinking that they have this pigeon just where they want him, and then take Chet under their wing to "help him out." Of course, that's usually just when Chet has them where he wants them. In the course of their explaining the deal to Chet, the others often reveal much more than they'd care to about their own needs and what they'd be willing to concede.

After awhile, Chet knows a whole lot more about them and what they want, must have, and can afford to give away than they do about him. In fact, they usually know nothing at all about him or his thinking. So, when he kind of smiles self-consciously and says with humility, "Shucks, I don't really know if this is a fair offer so you tell me because you know a whole lot more about these things than I do, but why don't you give up this...and this...which you just said you don't care about and take this...and this...which you just said you want and maybe then we can all shake hands and go home?" they are often taken completely by surprise.

Tip

Watch out for anyone who starts out by saying, "Shucks...." There is no real meaning for this word! It's just a cover for establishing the role of an innocent. And in real estate negotiations there are very few innocents left.

Sarah was a real estate investor with more than 30 years of solid experience. Yet she never came into negotiations bragging about her knowledge. In fact, she tried to conceal it in a most unusual way. She would feign deafness in one ear.

Have you ever noticed what happens when a hearing-impaired person is trying to understand what's being said? Everyone around suddenly speaks not only louder and slower, but also in easier-to-understand terms. Yet the person is only hard of hearing, not stupid.

Once I was present when Sarah was negotiating to buy a duplex. She had been presented as a tough negotiator, and the seller was obviously worried about how big a price concession he would have to make.

Sarah simply came in, shook hands, and presented an offer for $125,000. The seller had been asking $137,000. It was a significant $12,000 price reduction.

The seller put up a good show and said, "My price is $137,000."

But every time the seller told her his price, Sarah would lean forward and say, "What?" The seller would repeat the price, only somehow each time it was just a little bit lower.

"What?"

"I said my price was $137,000," the seller repeated, "but I am willing to drop it down to $135,000 to make the deal."

"What?"

"That's $135,000. I said I was willing to take $135,000. Of course, I suppose I could go lower."

"What?"

"I said I could go lower, maybe $134,000."

"What?"

"Oh, all right. My bottom price is $130,000. I can't afford to go any lower than that."

"What?"

The seller picked up the offer, looked at the $125,000 bid, shook his head, and simply signed.

I always wondered just how low that seller might have gone if Sarah had continued to "What?" her way through the negotiations!

Trap

Most of us are too eager to show off just how much we know. This can work against us. For example, what if the other party says that since we're acting as the expert we should explain how to proceed? If we jump into the breach, we can often reveal too much too soon about what we're willing to give up to get the deal. We must let go of the ego-satisfying position of know-it-all and instead assume the profit-making position of innocent.

Tip

Ask others for their advice. Invite their criticism. Be willing to have them analyze your offer. This will make you look humble and needing of help. Say something like "This is what I want. But perhaps I don't fully understand. Maybe there's something about this deal that needs to be explained. Could you please enlighten me?" In their rush to criticize, advise, and analyze, your "opponents" will trip over themselves revealing what it is they really want and how far they are willing to go to get it. All that it costs to learn about your opponents is a little humility.

RULE 8—Always Ask "Why?"

Sometimes seemingly impossible demands will threaten to shut down a deal. For example, you're a buyer and the seller keeps insisting that you be ready to fund your new mortgage within 21 days. You've already contacted a mortgage broker and know that it's going to take a month or more, given the volume of loans being processed at that time. You say you need longer, but the seller keeps hitting you over the head with that 3-week limitation. No, she won't give you more time. The demand is sucking the energy right out of the deal.

To keep things alive, you may say you'll try to get qualified in 3 weeks, even though you know full well it's impossible. You're hoping that after the time is up, the seller will give you some more time.

Instead, you could simply ask the seller, "Why are you insisting on 21 days?"

"Why?" is often the biggest single weapon in a negotiation. Yet many people are simply afraid to ask. I suspect they don't want to know the answer for fear it will ruin the deal entirely. Maybe there's an absolutely immutable reason the seller must have 21 days. And as soon as you hear it, you'll know the deal is blown away. But isn't it better to know up-front where you stand than to wait 3 weeks to find out? Besides, there are very few absolutely immutable reasons.

The seller may say, "I've got a backup offer and if you don't qualify, I'll take it." Now, at least, you know what you've got to deal with. Asking why has revealed the problem and maybe there's a solution. Perhaps you could show the seller your credit report and a letter from the lender saying you are well qualified. Yes, your deal will go through, but you need 4 weeks instead of 3. Maybe you could increase the deposit.

The point is, if you don't ask "Why?" you won't find out. If you do, chances are you'll learn useful information.

Let's consider a different example. The buyer insists on a price lower than market, even though as a seller you've already offered to sell for what recent comparables have gone for. Instead of continuing to argue, you simply ask, "Why do you really insist on such a low price?"

Again, you might not like the answer. Perhaps the buyer would say, "My brother bought a house for that price in this neighborhood 2 years ago. I'm not paying more."

You might point out that 2 years ago the area was in recession. Today it's recovering and prices are higher. But chances are that this buyer's real desire is not to be "bettered" by her sibling and won't budge. Now it really is a brick wall you're up against.

However, a person who finds price all-important is often more than willing to dicker on the terms. You might ask the buyer to give you a second mortgage at an interest rate well above market. If he does that, maybe it's worth your while to give him his price. You get terms that make a lower price worthwhile to you.

Of course, it never would happen unless you asked "Why?"

One problem with the "Why?" question is that as negotiations get tougher, the other party is less and less inclined to be forthright in answering. When asked "Why?" in the middle or end of a negotiation, most people are immediately suspect of the question and the questioner. Is the other party trying to learn information that will create an edge? Why should one side say anything that might give the other side ammunition for getting a better deal?

Trust is now all-important. If you've established trust early on, if you've stuck to the high moral road, you probably will get a straight answer. If not, asking "Why" in the middle or end of a negotiation will probably produce a guarded answer.

Tip

Most people are afraid to reveal their true motivations. Asking "Why?" may get them out into the open. However, many times it is a mistake to conceal your true motivations. If other people know what you truly want, they may be able to give it to you.

Trap

Sometimes you do want to keep your motivations to yourself. Maybe you've learned that a new commercial center is going in next to a store you want to buy, and the center will double the store's value. To reveal your motivation will cause the seller to refuse the deal or to increase the price.

RULE 9—Question Authority

"Question authority" is a phrase out of the 1960s when the flower children believed that everyone over 30 was the enemy. Of course, all the flower children are now over 40 or 50, so I suppose the phrase no longer applies in a sociological setting. But it does have a special meaning in real estate.

When you're negotiating, other people may sometimes take all the energy out of a deal with their "authority." If you let them continue, they could kill the deal.

For example, I was recently involved in the sale of a home near the coastline. The buyer's agent kept insisting that the seller should lower the price because the house was run down and small and the Coastal Commission would prevent any buyer from improving the property. The seller wasn't going to lower the price and I could see the life slipping out of the deal. I had to reenergize it.

I wasn't that familiar with the Coastal Commission's regulations, although I did know that the agency was very strict in regard to anyone building within its jurisdiction. But, I suspected, it was not as strict as the buyer's agent portrayed. So I challenged her, saying I didn't think the buyer would be precluded from improving anything on the inside of the property and probably could add on to the outside, but with a permit.

She immediately said I was wrong, that I didn't know the rules (which technically was true) and that she did because she handled properties in this area all the time. Now there was a decision to be made. Either the seller and I could accept her as the authority or we could challenge further. We decided to take it another step. I called the Coastal Commission and was referred to a local attorney who handled a lot of cases involving the agency's rulings. After contacting the attorney, we discovered that yes, indeed, the regulations were strict, but the kinds of changes that this buyer wanted to make would probably be allowed without much difficulty. Suddenly the buyer's arguments for a lower price disappeared—and the seller got a better deal.

When it's the authority that is causing you a problem in a deal, challenge. Usually the worst you can do is discover that the authority is right. But the best is often to find out that the authority is wrong.

Finding an Alternate Authority. Sometimes the authority is only voicing an opinion. For example, you may be involved in a transaction in which the critical factor is whether the buyer will qualify for a mortgage. If the buyer qualifies, the deal will go through because both parties are agreed on price and other terms. But if the buyer doesn't qualify, there's no deal.

The seller's agent may call up a mortgage broker who, when given the facts regarding the buyer's credit, down payment, income, and other qualifications, comes to the conclusion that the buyer isn't going to make it. Suddenly the deal's history—unless you can counter the "authority." So you call up a different mortgage broker (assuming you're the buyer), hopefully one with whom you've already made arrangements for securing financing, and she now says that, yes, you will qualify for the needed loan and that she will fund it.

Suddenly things look up. Your authority is better, presumably, than the one the seller's agent called, because yours is willing not only to say you qualify but also to make the loan. If your mortgage broker puts it all in writing, you could have a solid deal.

Challenging the Authority's Credentials. There are many different cases in which you'll want to challenge an authority's credentials. One of these may be when you are getting a hard time by someone who, you suspect, shouldn't be butting in at all.

For example, not long ago an escrow officer kept calling me up and insisting that I produce certain documents, claiming that they were essential to the transaction. At first, I complied simply to get the deal done, with the least amount of hassle. But when I was asked to come up with a birth certificate, driver's license, social security number, and bank reference, I balked. The escrow officer said these were necessary to identify me in the transaction and to be sure that the check I submitted for the purchase was valid.

Trap

In the past, if you were a buyer, simply putting a cashier's check into escrow was usually considered sufficient for completing a deal. However, in recent years some unscrupulous people have devised ways of canceling their cashier's checks and some escrows and title insurance companies have been burned, transferring title and issuing their own payment checks only to find that the buyer's cashier's check had bounced. (Believe it; it does happen!) As a consequence, today escrow agents often require additional safeguards, usually in the form of time—the cashier's check must be deposited 24 or 48 hours prior to the close of escrow so it has time to clear.)

I understood the escrow officer's concerns, but realized that he was going overboard. So I said no. I'd supply a driver's license and social security number, if necessary, and deposit the cashier's check ahead of the close of escrow. That was it.

The escrow officer said that wasn't sufficient.

I replied that the escrow officer was simply there to fulfill the wishes of the parties concerned and had no authority to demand more. If he kept insisting, I'd be forced to change escrows, even at that late date.

The escrow officer was furious and called the title insurance company (to which I was well known) and the seller. The escrow officer called back an hour later, saying that he had "smoothed things out" and that the extra documents weren't necessary after all.

Beware of people who are officious, especially those who feel that it is their duty to create rules and build barriers because of their apparent position of authority. In the final analysis, they may not have the credentials to make their demands stick.

RULE 10—Challenge the Written Word

Have you ever noticed the power of the printed word? You're signing a lease that reads "No Pets Allowed." You have a pet. Suddenly you feel the energy flowing out of the agreement. You won't get rid of Bowser, and the landlord won't take pets.

Can you keep the deal alive?

Certainly. Just remember that whoever wrote out the agreement decided that as a general rule, pets were not desirable and a good way of discouraging tenants from having them was to include those words. An agent can point to the sentence as proof that pets aren't allowed. You, of course, could simply cross out the word "No" and initial your change. If the landlord wanted you as a tenant, he or she might initial it too. Then Bowser would be allowed.

Written words have uncommon power to affect our lives. You go to a movie theater and after buying your ticket see a sign that says "Line Forms Here." So you stand there. But what if you stood somewhere else and people stood behind you? Then the sign would be wrong, wouldn't it?

Often a mortgage application will note on one or more papers that you, the borrower, are asked to sign that you must pay for a whole list of fees, including:

Document drawing

Document transferal

Application submission fee

Notarization

These are, by and large, garbage fees that mortgage brokers and some lender's representatives use to pad the profits they make from the loan. But because it's printed on paper, most borrowers simply acquiesce without a question.

But you know that these are garbage fees and you don't want to pay them. Again, you feel the energy flowing away. Either you agree and feel cheated or you disagree and walk out.

There is another alternative: challenging the fees. All these fees are challengeable and negotiable. Just because they are written down on a paper you are asked to sign doesn't mean they are nonnegotiable.

Tip

When someone says that something is "nonnegotiable," what that may really mean is negotiations have just begun.

Tell the lender you want the loan, but you know these fees aren't reasonable and you want them removed or reduced. After the lender gets over his or her shock, negotiation may open. Of course, some lenders really won't dicker, particularly when they are making lots of loans. But in a slow market, many will.

Real estate documents—leases, sales agreements, options, listings—are rife with phrases that tell you what you can and cannot do. These are often called "boilerplate," because they regularly occur in every document. The trouble, of course, is that sometimes they are disadvantageous to you. For example, I once examined a sales agreement from a builder that required me to pay a minimum deposit of $5000 with the offer. In other words, I had to come up with $5000 in earnest money if I wanted to make an offer on the property.

I simply didn't want to come up with $5000. The printed word could kill the deal.

I wrote out a check for $500 and presented it to the agent. She smiled and said I had left off a zero. I said I hadn't. She pointed to the sentence. I took her pen and crossed the sentence out, then handed her back the check for $500. She didn't smile, but she also didn't refuse to present the offer.

A friend of mine once sought to list his property for sale. The agent's listing agreement had written in that the commission was 7 percent. He told the agent that he was willing to pay only 4 percent.

The agent said he was sorry, but he worked only for 7 percent. My friend replied that if that was the case, he would get another agent. Eventually they compromised at 5 percent.

Tip

Just because it's written doesn't mean it's true. If writing it down made it so, then everything you read in the newspapers would be gospel.

Make Lists. There is a corollary to this rule—namely, that you can use the written word to your advantage. You can use the written word to add energy to a deal. When I'm presenting an offer (or having one presented to me), I like to draw up lists. I ask the buyer (or the buyer's agent) to write down everything he or she wants out of the deal. I make a similar list myself and hand it to the other party. Of course, there are the usual things that pop up, such as price and monthly payment amount. But there can often be unexpected things, such as "home appearance," "good neighborhood," "number of bathrooms," and even "quick deal."

The list helps everyone identify what the real stumbling blocks may be. Maybe we've spent hours arguing about price. But what the buyer is really concerned about is neighborhood. If I convince the buyer that the neighborhood is really better than she thinks, she may be willing to pay a higher price. "But I'm really concerned with price," the buyer may say. My reply: "Indeed, then how come the first thing on your list is 'neighborhood'?" When it's written down, it's hard to deny.

If "quick deal" shows up anywhere on a buyer's list, I know that I'm almost home free. I simply say, "Okay, if I'm willing to sign right now and let you move in next week, will you accept my price and terms?" I may not get everything I want this way, but I usually can get a lot of it.

Putting it in writing helps identify the true needs and wants of the other party, needs that may not come out any other way. It also helps the other side to identify your true needs and wants. A list is a wonderful means of uncovering the triggers that will make your opponent move on the deal. And presenting a list from your perspective may help the other party give you just what you want.

RULE 11—Listen Carefully

Most of us listen to *how* a person talks more than to what he or she says. If people speak in a loud and angry voice, their anger, frustration, and perhaps fear come through. If they speak very softly, we may suspect that they are very calculating and even dishonest. People talking in a normal tone may lull us to sleep as we lose our concentration. And people speaking with obvious conviction may convince us of their forthrightness.

The point here, however, is that no matter what the delivery, it's often the words that count. Many times you can reenergize a deal, or get negotiations moving, simply by understanding what's really said. Here are some examples:

"Here's our *first offer*."

This always implies that a second, third, or other better offer is to come. When I hear this phrase, I automatically feel the energy flowing because I know that if I reject it, the second offer will be made.

"This is our *initial bid.*"

Again, better things are to come (see above).

"Here's *something* to get negotiations back on track."

This is a concession. Why is the other party offering a concession without receiving something in return unless he or she is more desperate to get the deal than I am? I will accept the concession and then see what happens next.

"Let's get things *out on the table.*"

This implies that I'm going to see only the negotiating position, not the final offer. The other side is presenting what he or she wants me to see. Now I'll reveal what I want that party to see. Then we'll get to it.

"This is our *first and final* offer."

Maybe, but only a fool issues an ultimatum at the start of negotiations. Is the other party really stupid? Or am I simply being stampeded into giving concessions? Now is when I should get the other side to invest time in the deal. (See Rule 18.)

"This is the *best* offer we can make."

Come on now; everyone can always do better. Real estate agents typically make this comment about their clients. What it usually means is that this is the offer the agent got without a lot of hassle. It's often a prelude to real concessions and negotiations.

"*Take it or leave it!*"

This ultimatum is usually issued after lengthy negotiations. Unless it's a ploy to force action on my part, it usually means that the other side is frustrated and has decided to give up the deal rather than continue trying to come up with something mutually acceptable. If I take it, I usually lose. If I leave it, we both usually lose. The better course is to ask for a short break, then come back and note areas of agreement, identify those of disagreement, and find a spot where some negotiation seems possible.

I think you get the idea. The words used by the other party are very revealing, if only you listen to them. Beware of delivery; listen closely to content.

Tip

If you listen closely enough, you'll discover everything the other party really wants out of the deal.

Sometimes it's not just the specific words themselves, but their sum total. Suppose I am a buyer asking a seller to carry back a second mortgage on the property. The buyer must have this second mortgage to make the deal. However, the seller offers questions such as these:

"Is the interest rate high *enough?*"

"What if you lose your job and *can't make* the payments?"

"During the last recession there were a lot of *defaults* on second mortgages, weren't there?"

"I hear that sellers are often *cheated* by creative financing."

What is this seller saying? For one thing, she's not saying that she doesn't want a second mortgage. If she didn't want a second mortgage, she would decline. Instead, in each statement she's saying, "Yes...but." It's the "but" that I need to address.

If I simply react without listening to what's actually being said, I might respond to each question in this fashion:

"The interest rate is as high as the market will bear."

"I've been on my job for 5 years and prospects look good."

"Yes, there were a lot of defaults, but the recession is ending."

"Creative financing isn't always bad—sometimes it's a good way to make a deal."

Have I responded in a way that will get the seller to go along? I suspect not. If I listen closer to what the seller is saying, I might perceive that she is really concerned that she will lose a lot of money or be cheated by taking a second mortgage. When she asks if the interest rate is high "enough," she's asking not about the market rate, but about whether it's enough to warrant the personal risk to her. When she asks if I "can't make" the payments, she doesn't want to hear about my job. She wants to know that I'll make the payments no matter what. When she asks about "defaults," she wants to know what's going to happen to her if I don't pay. And "cheated" suggests she doesn't trust anything that I'm saying about this subject.

The words reveal the true problem. What the seller really needs is to be reassured. What will reassure her? One sure thing is for me to increase my credibility as a borrower. For example, perhaps I could get some financially well-established party (such as my parents, a wealthy relative, or even the broker) to cosign. Or I could increase my credibility by putting more money down.

Once I've done something such as this to reassure the seller of my credibility, the arguments (in the form of questions) that she's raised melt away. She might even be willing to give me a lower-than-market interest rate and be sufficiently unconcerned about payments, defaults, or cheating to make concessions elsewhere.

What I have to do is listen to the words and discover the true concerns they reveal. Once I address these concerns, the superficial problems will dissolve.

Listen to the words. They will usually tell you what the other party really wants.

3
Strategies for Success

Everyone always talks about planning ahead. We're all supposed to plan ahead, but who ever does?

In negotiating, however, planning ahead means something a little bit different and actually something quite a bit easier. Here planning is having a strategy. Not a specific strategy just for the deal involved, but a general plan that you can always keep in mind.

- PEOPLE (How to handle those with whom you deal)
- TACTICS (Maneuvers that gain an advantage)
- **STRATEGY (Having one)**
- TIME (Getting it on your side)

Strategic Rules

RULE 12—Always Give Yourself an Alternative

RULE 13—Be Informed

RULE 14—Work Only on Issues That Can Be Resolved

RULE 15—Never Respond to an Offer That Can't Be Closed

RULE 16—Don't Stick to the "Pie" Analogy or "Bottom Line" Reasoning

RULE 17—Remember That Some Deals Can't Be Made, No Matter What

RULE 12—Always Give Yourself an Alternative

This rule is all about leverage in negotiation. If you follow it, you'll have leverage. If you don't, you will not get the deal you want because you won't have the leverage necessary to get it.

The classic example here is of a young couple who go out to buy their first home. They are shown dozens of properties until one day they run across one that's simply perfect. It's got location—close to shopping, in a safe neighborhood, and near schools. The house has the right number of bedrooms and bathrooms. The design of the kitchen is perfect; the arrangement of the rooms, delightful. In short, it's the one house of their dreams. And therein lies the rub.

Our couple have found the right house, the perfect house, the one and only house and they have no alternative. Thus, when the seller asks $9000 more than its market value, what are they to do?

Yes, they can bluff and offer less. But even this option is limited, because they fear that someone will come in with a higher offer and snatch the house out from under them. Thus, when the seller rejects a first lower offer, the young couple—not wanting to lose this perfect property—give the seller exactly what she wants not only in price, but in terms as well.

In short, the buyers have no leverage with which to negotiate. They have to have the house; consequently, they have to pay the price.

On the other hand, consider a more mature couple who have bought and sold a number of homes. They are now looking for their next home and in the process they identify three houses within a given neighborhood that are all suitable. They pick the best of the lot and make an offer, perhaps $12,000 less than the asking price.

When the seller counters with only $1000 less than he's asking, the couple doesn't at all feel they have to take the offer or lose out on the one and only property of their dreams. They know there are two other perfectly good houses waiting for their offer. So they tell the seller that either he can take their original offer or they'll look elsewhere. Further, they give him only 24 hours to decide.

Suddenly the seller realizes that if he's going to sell to this couple, he'll have to lower his sights. If the market's tough (as it has been over the past few years in many areas), if there haven't been any other buyers (in other words, the seller doesn't have any alternatives), and if he needs to get out, he may indeed take the buyer's lowball offer. At the least, he's likely to make a more realistic counter.

Tip

Houses are like love. Either you believe there is one and only one perfect mate for you in the whole world or you come to realize that you can be perfectly happy with hundreds, perhaps thousands, of different people who are all "just right," if you can find them. Similarly, you can believe there is only one perfect house in the world for you. Or you can be more pragmatic and realize that there are dozens, even hundreds, of homes in which you could be perfectly happy. The pragmatic person can negotiate. The perfectionist has to pay the price that's asked.

The need for alternatives applies not only to the purchase of a home but also to all aspects of real estate—whether it's finding suitable financing, negotiating a lease, or simply paying a deposit. If you give yourself options, you will be in a position to negotiate. If you leave yourself no alternatives, you are more likely to have to accept whatever the other party offers.

RULE 13—Be Informed

Tip

The old maxim "Knowledge is power" applies doubly in real estate.

Being informed can make a big difference in almost every sale. For example, you're presenting an offer that contains a financing contingency which specifies that the purchase is subject to your obtaining a mortgage at 90 percent of value. (You're putting 10 percent down.)

As soon as you present your offer, the agent for the seller says, "You can't get that loan because you're not planning to live in the property. Only buyers who intend to live in the home can get a 90 percent loan. The best investors can get is 80 or maybe 75 percent. Either come up with more down or you've got no deal!"

Now, do you look wide-eyed, confused, and slightly embarrassed by this turn of events? If you do, then you haven't done your homework. Further, you're not going to be able to successfully negotiate here, unless you come up with a lot more money—which you probably don't want to do (or are unable to do). The problem is, you don't know the right answer.

Did You Do Your Homework? You should have previously contacted lenders to find out if a nonowner-occupied purchase would qualify for 90 percent financing. (It almost never does!) If there's no financing available, then you should have structured your offer differently, perhaps with a 75 percent first loan and a 15 percent second loan from the seller.

Or you should have found a lender willing to give you a nonoccupant 90 percent mortgage. (A few do exist in some areas.)

If you had done your homework and been properly informed, when challenged by the seller's agent, you could have simply smiled and whipped out a letter from a lender promising to make you a 90 percent loan on the property. The seller's agent would now look foolish (instead of you) and you might be able to press for some other concessions, having thus established your authority.

Here's another scenario. You're a seller receiving an offer to purchase a property. The offer contains a contingency clause—a condition that must be met before the sale can be completed. The clause says, "Seller agrees to pay for all costs of repair or retrofitting as required by termite or other reports as required by lender, insurer, or state."

Now, should you sign a contract with this contingency in it or not? You probably know that virtually all lenders require at least a termite report clearance before they will fund a mortgage for the buyer. Also, in almost all locales the seller is expected to pay for correcting all damage. You're prepared for this. But are there any other reports that are required? If so, they could add up to a lot of money and you may want to delete the condition. If not, and the buyer is just being cautious, you may want to go ahead and sign. The question is one of knowledge.

Many people, figuring the contingency applies only to a termite report and clearance for which they have to pay anyway, would sign. However, in some areas today there are additional requirements being made by the lender, insurer, or state. For example, some states may soon require that an earthquake, hurricane, or cyclone report be issued and that a clearance showing that the house is protected from these disasters be given prior to sale. The costs here can be extremely high—perhaps $10,000 per house or more.

Did You Investigate Before You Signed?　The lender may require a special report on flooding because you are in a flood plain as well as a clearance showing that certain expensive retrofitting steps have been taken to protect your home. Or a fire insurance company may require a report on roofs in your area because of an extreme fire hazard where your property is located. The insurer may also insist on a clearance saying that your roof is of fireproof materials. (Replacing an old wood shingle roof with fireproof shingles or tiles can easily cost $10,000 or more.)

Trap

Some sellers simply don't realize that everything in an offer is negotiable, including the contingencies. If you don't like the contingencies, you can rewrite them. Of course, your changes nullify the offer and now you must get the buyer to accept the changes. But that's all part of the negotiation.

Today the whole world of real estate transactions is complicated by the demands of a host of companies and agencies that are external to the transaction. However, if you're unaware of

what's required of you in your area, your ignorance could cost
you a fortune. If you sign a clause saying you'll pay, then you'll
have to pay.

Tip

Although signed sales agreements are supposed to be binding,
in actual practice often the language in them is flawed or the
sellers or buyers can claim they were not properly informed
about the consequences of their actions by their agents or attor-
neys. Thus, another useful bit of knowledge is that just because
you signed, you're not necessarily on the hook. Extenuating circumstances just *might* save your rear end. Only you can't count
on this. It's far better to have the knowledge not to sign a bad
agreement than to sign and have to try to get out of it later.

The key here is to be informed. Having knowledge of perti-
nent facts can often mean the difference between negotiating a
winning or a losing deal.

RULE 14—Work Only on Issues That Can Be Resolved

Tip

Always do the possible first. Leave the impossible till later.

You're a buyer and you offer to purchase a home. You want
the seller to accept a lower price, carry a second mortgage,
move out within 30 days, and put on a new roof.

When the seller looks at this offer, his first inclination is to
throw it and you out the door.

But you want to buy and he wants to sell. So you suggest that
first you both identify any issues which can be resolved and
separate them from those which can't.

Price comes up immediately. He doesn't want to accept what you are offering, but indicates he will negotiate something lower than he's asking. There is a possible resolution here.

Next he mentions that he doesn't want to put on a new roof. But he knows that old roof is bad and is willing to patch it. Maybe that's negotiable too.

However, he flat out says he cannot move out in 30 days. He simply can't. His kids are in school for another 2½ months. He would have to find another place to live and he's going to be traveling for the next month, so he won't have time to look. It's simply not possible.

This issue is intractable.

Further, he says he needs cash, so no way will he consider a second mortgage. Again intractable.

Now, are you going to focus on the time factor and the second mortgage? Or on the roof and the price? If you turn to the time factor, he says, "No, no, no." If you turn to the issue of the second mortgage, again he says, "No, no, no." Suddenly it appears as if everything is wrong and there's no way to move forward. In fact, you've just lost the deal because you've brought negotiations to a halt.

On the other hand, if you instead concentrate on the two issues that may be possible to resolve, maybe you can make some progress. So you work with the seller on the roof. No, he doesn't want to replace it, but he concedes that it is bad. Eventually you both agree that he'll put on a new roof, but a less inexpensive one.

You both heave a sigh of relief. Things are going better. You've just resolved a big issue. The time you've both invested has paid off. You're both optimistic. So you now tackle price.

Your offer is too low, the seller says. But he concedes that he has some room to maneuver. "How much room?" you ask. You continue to negotiate into the wee hours of the night and finally hit upon a price that both of you consider reasonable. Again a collective sigh of relief is expressed. You both feel you're much closer to a deal.

But, you point out, you can't meet that price unless the seller gives you a second mortgage. You don't have the extra cash. But, he says, he must have the cash in order to buy the next house.

So you put your heads together to see what you can work out. You suggest that he take the second mortgage and sell it to an investor. No, he won't get full price for it. But if you're a good credit risk (and you surely indicate you are), if the interest rate is high enough, and if the term is short enough, couldn't he convert it to cash somewhere? His ears perk up. Maybe there is a way.

He remembers an uncle with a lot of cash who's looking for solid investments. He rousts his uncle out of bed even though it's 1:30 at night, makes effusive apologies for the late call, and then explains the problem. The uncle, convinced of the severity of the problem by the late-hour call, but always looking for a good deal and liking his nephew, agrees. He'll sign off in the morning.

You both shake hands. It appears you've got the deal. "Oh, by the way," you mention. "I still need to move in within 30 days."

"No problem," says the seller. "I'll move out and rent temporarily." The deal is done.

But why is it done?

The answer is that it's human nature to "go with the flow," to follow the trend. The word is *momentum*. Get it on your side and you can make a seemingly impossible deal.

You can see this most clearly in football games. You may have two evenly matched teams, but if one gains momentum by quickly building up a lead, the game may blow out and become a mismatched contest. Similarly, in a real estate deal, once movement begins to occur, once you have agreement on some issues, the tendency is to want to continue the momentum, to continue finding agreement. (By contrast, if there were no momentum, the tendency would be to feel the deal had no chance of being made.) Agreement begets agreement—it's positive action. In the end, an issue such as when to give occupancy, which is intractable at the beginning, seems trivial after everything else that's been accomplished.

Tip

If you work first on those issues which you can resolve, those which you can't may take care of themselves.

Remember, if you begin by trying to negotiate an impossible issue, you are doomed to failure. So why bother? Instead, work on those issues which you can resolve. Maybe, just maybe, by the time you've successfully worked out several issues, the other party will have enough familiarity with and confidence in you and in the negotiating process to make concessions that seemed impossible hours earlier.

Trap

Some readers unfamiliar with just how real estate deals are put together may not believe anyone would make a call at 1:30 in the morning asking for money, much less get it. Believe it! When a seller (or buyer) is hot to close a deal, he or she will do almost anything to make the deal work.

RULE 15—Never Respond to an Offer That Can't Be Closed

Here comes a real estate classic. You're a seller and are asking $100,000 for your property. A buyer comes through your house, looks at it, leaves and, comes back again the next day. You're sure this person is interested and after talking awhile she says, "Would you take $80,000 for your property?"

You're anxious to sell and you reply, "No, no I wouldn't, but I'd look favorably at $90,000!"

You've just committed a no-no. You've started negotiations on a deal that can't be concluded. Why can't it be concluded? Because there's no formal offer on the table. The would-be buyer hasn't offered anything. She has simply asked a question.

In effect, you've just given away $10,000 before the negotiations have even begun. If this would-be buyer eventually makes an offer, you can be darned sure it's going to be predicated on a $90,000 asking price, not the $100,000 you purportedly want.

What should you have said? That's easy. When the wannabe buyer asks, "Would you take $80,000 for your property?" The correct reply is, "Are you offering $80,000?"

The would-be buyer might now fall back and regroup. "Well, let's say that I do? Would you consider it?"

This is merely a restatement of the first question. You now need to restate your response.

"Put your offer in writing, enclose an earnest money deposit, present it to me, and I'll let you know."

The point is that you should respond only to a legitimate offer that can be closed. If it can't be closed, then true negotiations haven't really started.

Tip

Your goal is to get the other party to the negotiating table. Until an offer is made, you've got nothing to negotiate.

It's very important to understand that in real estate verbal offers can be made and, indeed, in very rare circumstances verbal *agreements* can be made (though not usually enforced). However, this is the unusual exception, not the rule. The traditional method used 99+ percent of the time is the formal offer in writing. This should be accompanied by a deposit (called "earnest money" because, quite simply, it shows the buyer is in earnest). Once the written offer with deposit is made, negotiations are under way. Until then, there's nothing on the table, no way to conclude negotiations. Therefore, you shouldn't begin to deal.

This problem can crop up at any time. For example, you've made an offer to a seller and are hot in negotiations. Along the way the seller suddenly says, "What if we just table this for awhile? I think you need to go back and rethink your offer and I need to sleep on it."

Trap

You don't "table" real estate negotiations. Either you've got a deal or you don't.

What the seller is actually proposing here is to stop negotiations. In effect, he's making an offer that can't be closed.

If you accept, you allow your offer to continue in force indefinitely while the seller neither accepts nor rejects it. In other words, he's asking for an open-ended offer on your part. If a better offer comes in over the course of the next few days or weeks, he's free to take it. (By the way, in real estate, all offers are presented as they arrive. Even if you have an offer pending, if another is made, it is, or should be, presented immediately.) The seller here has nothing to lose if you agree. He's, in effect, offering you nothing.

The point, of course, is that the seller is making an open-ended offer that can't be closed. Your response should be immediate and clear. You might say something like this: "I understand what you're saying. But I'm looking to buy property today and I have several pieces I'm considering. I believe we should continue negotiations until they are concluded. If you break them off, I'll assume that's a rejection and look elsewhere." In a friendly manner, indicate that you have alternatives and lead the negotiations back toward a conclusion.

RULE 16—Don't Stick to the "Pie" Analogy or "Bottom Line" Reasoning

Some time in the distant past there was an unlucky baker who said, "I've got only so many pieces of pie to sell and when they're gone, I'll close for the day." Soon after, "pie charts" came into existence for demonstrating how the total amount of a transaction could be distributed. The world was quickly locked into an unfortunate analogy. When it became common practice to speak of this as the "bottom line," meaning the last position to be taken on a deal, negotiation took a giant step backward. We looked at the pie concept in the introduction to this book. Now let's expand by tackling the conceptual part of this problem first.

The Problem with Pie.   On the surface, the pie analogy appears to be sound. A deal, any deal, has only so much money (or property or conditions or whatever). That means that, like a pie, it can be cut only into so many pieces. Each person in the deal can get a big slice or a small slice. But when all the slices are handed out, the pie is gone.

You want to buy a home, but you're offering much less than the seller is asking. When you present the deal and begin negotiating, the seller brings up the pie analogy. She says, "You're offering $200,000 for the property. I have to pay a 6 percent commission, or $12,000. I have a $150,000 first mortgage and a $30,000 second mortgage. That leaves me only $8000 out of which to pay closing costs. By the time the deal is done, I won't have any money left at all! I won't sign."

As long as you hold to the pie analogy, the seller is perfectly correct and there's no deal to be made here. However, why not throw the pie back at the baker and work creatively? What about the furniture? Maybe there's some nice furniture in the house that originally cost the seller $10,000. But she's moving to an apartment and doesn't have room for most of it. Indeed, she's tired of it and would be happy to sell it. So you offer an additional $5000 for the furniture. She's happy to get rid of it and now she's got some cash. In addition, you up the price to $205,000 and, if the lender concurs, you finance the cost so it's only pennies a month out of your pocket. The pie's gotten bigger.

Maybe the seller has other assets—a recreational vehicle, for example. You've always wanted one of these; indeed, you'd planned on buying one. So instead of buying just property, you buy the property and the vehicle. The seller gets more cash, which is what she wants, and you get something you would have bought anyway. The pie's growing again.

The real estate agent wants to make the deal. But maybe there's no deal without some creative concessions. So instead of $12,000 in cash, you ask the agent to take $5000 in cash and a second mortgage on another property owned by the seller. She pays the agent off a little each month, but gets to keep $7000 in cash for herself.

The pie's bigger still.

Trap

Don't expect a real estate agent to automatically offer to discount a commission by taking back paper (mortgage) instead of cash. Most agents won't want to do it. Many simply won't do it at all. But creative agents who do a lot of business and who see the deal can't be made any other way often will. It's usually a last resort. When it works, it can make the deal.

There's really no limit to how big you can grow the pie, once you stop seeing it as a limiting analogy.

Bottom Lining. Now, let's move from the conceptual image of a pie to a specific application. Many people, particularly those who don't negotiate regularly, feel it's important to adopt a "bottom line." They see this as a safety precaution to keep them from committing too deeply or spending too much. It's like going to Las Vegas and saying, "We've got $300 to blow. When it's all gone, we quit." In other words, they are committing to a pie of a certain maximum size, in advance.

There's really nothing wrong with doing this. Indeed, as long as you understand the limitations, it's often a good idea. The real trouble with setting up a bottom line, however, is that you usually do it before you understand the whole deal. Once the entire deal is presented to you, you may find that the bottom line set is inappropriate.

For example, Peter and Sheila are selling their home. They're asking $95,000. However, they know that offers are most likely to come in for less. So, beforehand they discuss the minimum they'll accept. They decide it's $90,000. If they can't get $90,000, they won't sell.

There are two things wrong here. First, what if an offer comes in for $90,000? That's their bottom line. Do they accept the offer? Or do they hold out for more?

They are at a psychological disadvantage if they've already decided that $90,000 is their bottom line. They are thinking that here's an offer they can accept. If they counter, they are giving up this offer in the hope (perhaps vain hope) that they'll get more. Maybe it's better to take one offer in hand than two in the bush. Having already set up a bottom line, they are unlikely to counter and if they do, they counter weakly. In short, their bottom line may get them less than they might otherwise have received for their home.

On the other hand, let's say the offer comes in at $85,000. Now, they know they won't accept that offer no matter what. In fact, it's way off the mark and they may feel insulted. They may make only a token counter at $94,000, which could make the buyer feel it's hopeless and cause him or her to give up on the deal.

Or maybe they'll counter at their bottom line, $90,000. Now, when the buyer counters back at $87,500, what do they do? They've got nowhere to go. Here, their bottom line has restricted their flexibility to deal with a lowball offer.

On the other hand, let's say that Peter and Sheila did not set up a bottom line. The first offer comes in at $90,000. They might come back with a strong counter higher. They want the most they can get and are willing to negotiate for it.

What about an $85,000 offer? Maybe they'll examine the terms the buyer is offering. Perhaps there's a second mortgage for them with a very high interest rate that they like. Maybe, because of the terms, they'll accept $87,000 or $88,000 or even $85,000.

The point here is that if you set a bottom line in advance, you limit your ability to negotiate. It's like the pie analogy all over again. You've locked yourself in and have nowhere to go.

Trap

The bottom line is supposed to protect you from losing more than you want or can afford. However, just as often it keeps you from getting a deal or making more than you anticipated.

The simple truth is that you can't know what your true best bottom line is in advance. Only when you see the deal, its terms and ramifications, can you decide what's in your best interests. Therefore, my suggestion is that if you feel the need for a bottom line, make it tentative, not rigid.

Tip

Say to yourself, "This is what I'd like to get without seeing the deal. However, I'll rethink after I see the deal itself."

RULE 17—Remember That Some Deals Can't Be Made, No Matter What

I've been asked why I included this rule among my recommendations for successful negotiations. The reason is that unless you recognize in the back of your mind that sometimes the deal can't be made, you will miss out on some good deals.

Sometimes, but only after extensive, intensive, and forthright negotiation, it becomes clear that no matter what you do, you can't make a deal with the other party. You've gone through the rules and have not offended the other side, you're dealing with a person who has the power to negotiate, you've made lists, and you've disarmed psychological attacks. You've done it all. And after all of it, the deal just can't be made. You're too far apart in price or in terms. You've tried to compromise. You realize the other side has tried to compromise. The awful truth is that there just isn't a deal to be made here.

Once you realize this, the mistake is to continue negotiating. If you continue, you may give up something you can't afford to lose and may end up with a deal you're better off without.

Trap

What's worse than not making a deal? It's making a deal in which you lose.

So, what you do is you announce that you've tried your best. You've given it every bit of creative effort you have and you just don't see how any deal can be made between the two of you. So you're ending negotiations. If you're a buyer, you'll look for another house. If you're a seller, you'll look for another buyer.

At this point, your opponents have a decision to make. Either they can concur with you, shake hands, say there's no hard feelings, and leave, each of you to go your separate ways. Or they can make concessions that will make the deal more appealing to you. Why would they do this?

One reason may be that they've been giving you only their posture, their negotiating "position" and that they really do want to make this work more than they've let on. By walking away from the table, you've forced them out into the open.

Another reason may be that they've never read this book and simply don't know that sometimes it's better not to make the deal. They're determined to make the deal no matter what, even if it's to their disadvantage.

Trap

Sometimes people will walk away from negotiations as a ploy. It's not that they believe no deal can be made. They think they can pressure the other side into making concessions. However, if you walk away before concluding that there is no deal possible, if you do it as a ploy, how do you come back if the other side recognizes what you're doing and simply says, "Bye-bye"? If you still want the deal, now you have to come back, eat humble pie, and try again from an obviously weaker position.

The ultimate test of the other side is to conclude that there's no deal to be made and walk away. If they let you go, then you know that your assessment was correct. If, however, they rush after you urging you to come back to the table, then you now know that they've been only posturing, not really being fully open.

When you're called back, it's time to play hardball. You can say the obvious: "I walked away because I assumed there was nothing more to say or do. But your calling me back suggests that my understanding of what you have to offer was incorrect. What is new that you now bring to this deal that will cause me to continue with the negotiations?"

Often the other side will now present some new concession or creative plan. However, I have been at this position and had the opposite side simply reiterate its old position. As soon as it became apparent that nothing new was being offered, I walked away again. When the other party came after me once more, I simply said, "Put it in writing and I'll consider it," and left.

Trap

You can't negotiate successfully with people whose main hope of "winning" is simply to wear you down by keeping you at the table.

Tip

If you are dealing with a "wear 'em out" negotiator, do it at a distance. Get the other side to write it down on paper and submit it to you. You can then accept, reject, or modify. By maintaining distance, you have avoid having the other side gain an advantage by wearing you out.

4
Getting Time on Your Side

Time is always an essential part of every real estate transaction. In fact, the words "Time is of the essence" are frequently written into real estate contracts to emphasize just this.

What is surprising to many people, however, is that time is a partisan player. You can make it work for you or you can let the other side make it work against you. If you don't pay attention to time, at some point in the negotiations, probably to your surprise, you will suddenly find you're running out of time. The other side, however, is sitting back with all the time in the world.

- PEOPLE (How to handle those with whom you deal)
- TACTICS (Maneuvers that gain an advantage)
- STRATEGY (Having one)
- **TIME (Getting it on your side)**

Rules for Getting Time on Your Side

RULE 18—Get the Other Party to Invest Time

RULE 19—Set a Deadline

RULE 20—Act Quickly

**RULE 18—Get the Other Party to
Invest Time**

Tip

Time invested is almost as good as money invested.

Let's say you want to lease a house. But instead of the cus-
tomary 1-year lease, you want a lease for only 6 months. And
instead of taking the place "as is," you want the owner to paint
the house completely on the inside. And you have a dog and
three cats...and a water bed.

You get the idea. You've got a whole lot of extras that make
you a landlord's nightmare. How do you get the landlord to
accept you anyway?

Let's say you walk up to the owner and simply blurt it all out.
"I want to rent your house, but you have to repaint it, give me a
6-month lease instead of a full year, accept my pets and allow me
to keep a water bed, which could leak and ruin your property."

Now, how do you think the typical landlord is going to react?
If it were me, I would show you to the nearest door and not
breathe easy until you were long gone. (Just in case you've
never rented your premises, dogs, cats, and water beds are the
nemeses of landlords; the only thing worse is tenants who want
to stay only a short time.)

On the other hand, let's say you tried a different approach,
one involving time. You came to the landlord and indicated you
were interested in the property, but you weren't sure. You talked
with him awhile, not mentioning your extras, and you got to
know each other. Then you left.

Chances are he was favorably impressed by you and, all
things being equal, considered you a likely candidate for a tenant. He hoped you'd come back. (A landlord hates showing
property to people who have no intention of renting but are just
out "shopping," or to people whom the landlord would never
want as tenants—it's a complete waste of time.)

The next day you do come back and you say you're definitely
interested. The landlord is going to be pleased. At last he'll get

that empty (and costly) house off his hands. You further add that the rental amount is okay and you have excellent credit, which you're more than willing to let the landlord check out. Now the landlord is sure to be delighted. But, you mention, you want to be sure the property is just right. Could he tell you about the neighborhood, the schools, the shopping?

The landlord proceeds to spend the next 2 hours telling you about the marvelous environment around the rental. At the end of that time you appear duly impressed. You mention that you really are interested, but the place seems so dingy. Would he consider repainting it all?

The landlord might think to himself that he'd really rather not paint it. He might honestly think that it's probably rentable as is, or else he would have already painted it. On the other hand, during all that time spent talking, he's learned a lot about you. You've effectively presented yourself as a good catch as a tenant. While he would probably have said no if you had just walked up and asked him, now he's going to seriously consider acquiescing. The truth is, the time you and he have spent together has been well spent. Better a bird in the hand than half a dozen in the bush, he may think to himself. A good tenant, after all, is worth a paint job.

So he agrees to the painting and you say that as a consequence you're quite sure you want it, but you'll be back tomorrow with your husband. You want to make the final decision together. The landlord pretty much figures he's got the deal sewed up and makes arrangements with the painters.

Tomorrow you and your husband show up and go through the house all over again. The landlord's now pointing out how much nicer this room or that cabinet will look with new paint on it. He's already accepted repainting and it's no longer an issue. You ask the normal questions: how the heating system works, the air conditioning, the fireplace, the dishwasher, and other features. Time drags on. Finally, you say you'll take it. The landlord is very pleased.

However, you say you can accept only a 6-month lease. The landlord is not pleased. He has assumed all along that you would take a year's lease. He says he really wants to lease the property for a whole year. You nod that you understand, but point out that you're not sure just how long you're going to be in the area. You can guarantee only 6 months. If things work out, you could stay longer.

The landlord is thinking to himself that he should say no and wait for a tenant who will agree to stay longer. But if he doesn't accept you, he's got to start all over with someone else. Further, by now he's obtained a credit report and knows you're a good risk and probably will take good care of the place. And, he may rationalize, as you say, one never knows what will happen after 6 months. Maybe you'll stay another 6 months—or even longer. What it comes down to, finally, is whether or not he's going to throw away all that time and effort he's already expended on you when the only problem you offer is a shorter term. (By now, the issue of painting has receded into yesterday's problem.)

Tip

A concession once made, is almost impossible to take back.

You shake hands and sit down to write out the rental agreement. After going through the contract boilerplate, you come to the subject of pets. You say you have several pets, well behaved. Three are outdoor pets and one is a potty-trained indoor cat. The landlord grits his teeth and writes in the number "4" in the contract with regard to pets. He also adds several hundred dollars to the security deposit, to which you happily agree.

Finally, before signing off, he asks if you have a water bed. You innocently mention that you do, and ask if that's a problem. The landlord shakes his head and says, "I'll have to increase your deposit some more." You sigh and say that it's already high and you're quite sure the water bed is safe. It has never leaked and is of a special design that simply doesn't get holes. Okay, he says, worn out, and the agreement is signed.

Of course, in real life one never knows what any landlord will do. However, the point here is that as more and more time is spent on the negotiations, it becomes increasingly hard to dump the deal. If all the extras or problems are brought out at the beginning, it's so easy for the landlord to just say No! He's got nothing invested in you. You don't conform to his requirements. No is the easiest thing to say.

On the other hand, after 3 days of negotiating (all that time spent looking and thinking about the rental was negotiating whether either of you realized it or not), it's a different story. Now the landlord has a vested interest in finding a way to make it work. He wants you, so he'll paint. In the end, he really can't abide the pets. So he increases the deposit to make it work. If he had no time spent and didn't know you, the answer to both would surely have been no.

Tip

The more time invested in a deal, the more you've got to lose if it doesn't go through. Any time spent considering the deal always increases the chances of getting the other party to say yes.

Of course, this applies to all types of real estate transactions, not just rentals. I've sat with sellers and buyers into the wee hours of the night while they tried to decide whether to accept a particular condition (such as the interest rate on a mortgage, the date of occupancy, or even the price) of a sales offer. They might not like the condition, they might not want the condition, they might be inclined to refuse it. But after they've spent 6 hours or more discussing it, the thought of simply giving up without getting some kind of deal becomes abhorrent. In some cases, it actually become a challenge trying to figure out how to make it work. Thus, the sellers or buyers no longer simply wrestle with whether they want the particular condition in question, but instead worry over accepting that condition or losing everything. That there's something to lose comes from the fact that they have invested not money, but time.

Trap

Never be in a hurry when negotiating. The more time you get the other party to spend considering the deal, the more likely he or she is to accept your offer, regardless of what it is.

In my view, some of the very best "time negotiators" in real estate come from foreign countries, often in the third world, where bargaining is the rule rather than the exception. They are clear on the fact that true negotiation takes time and they are perfectly willing to spend lots of it to get what they want. They may drive you crazy with their technique, but more often than not, they get what they want.

RULE 19—Set a Deadline

If you've ever watched a telethon fund raiser, you quickly realize that 90 percent of the money is raised in the last hour. That's regardless of how long the telethon lasts, whether it be 5 hours or 50. It isn't until the drive gets down to the actual deadline that people contribute.

It's the same in journalism. Talk to any number of reporters and they will tell you that both their bane and their salvation is the deadline. They hate deadlines because of the pressure, yet they would never get a story written without them. (It also applies to writing books, as the publisher of this one will quickly tell you!)

Tip

No deal ever closes without a deadline.

It's even the same in basketball, at least at the professional level. Yes, in some games one side gets way out ahead and the outcome is never in doubt. But in many games, perhaps even most, the winner is decided in the last 2 minutes when both teams give it 110 percent.

The same is true in real estate. This is not to discount the element of time invested, as noted above, but deadlines are also crucial. (By the way, deadlines and "time invested" are not contradictions, but two sides of the same coin. Yes, you are far more likely to get what you want if you convince the other party to invest time. But you'll never get what you want until the deal closes and in most cases it won't close without a deadline.)

The best example I have seen of this is in the sales offer that a buyer makes to a seller. Usually the last consideration by the buyer is how long to give the seller to accept the offer. (Time is always of the essence in any deal and while it is possible to make an open-ended offer "until accepted"—very unwise as we shall see—most offers give the seller a specified time within which to accept.)

I have sat in with sales agents who advised their buyer clients, "Give the seller a week to think it over. He might go along with your deal."

That's a lot of hooey! In a week the seller may receive three other offers, two better than yours. Further, in a week the seller may have talked herself both into your offer and out of it again.

The best advice, in my opinion, is to set a deadline that forces the seller to invest time in considering the offer and then forces him or her to come up with a decision. In most cases, that's just one day, 24 hours.

I can hear the protests from those real estate agents who strongly believe in giving the other party plenty of time. But I stick to my guns. Setting a deadline, a realistic deadline, is the best way of getting your offer accepted. Here's why.

It's Enough Time. Assuming that the sellers can be reached, one day usually gives them plenty of time to consider the offer. If they begin looking at it by six o'clock, they should fully understand it by seven and they can chew it over through midnight. That's enough time for them to invest so that they will feel that if they simply reject the offer, they will have lost something (time invested).

Sellers Almost Never Accept First Offers. The theme of this book, after all, is negotiation and sellers usually see the initial offer for what it probably is, a "trial balloon," the first step in negotiations. While it's true that a seller who counters the offer has legally rejected it and given the buyer complete freedom to walk away from the deal, in most cases the buyer is looking for some sort of counter with which to work. In other words, the process of buying a property usually involves offer, counteroffer, counter-counteroffer, and so on. Thus, one way to get the seller or buyer to invest more time in a deal is with a series of counters. And the deadline helps makes this happen.

Procrastination Is Easier Than Action. Consider first the
seller's (or other party's) perspective. The seller has received an
offer. It's not right. The price is off, the terms are wrong. What is
the seller to do?

If there's no deadline, one appealing thing to do is nothing. If
the seller doesn't act, maybe the buyer will have a change of
heart and sweeten the offer. Further, if the seller waits, maybe
some other person will come in with a better offer. Putting off
making a decision, without a deadline, can often be the most
tempting route.

On the other hand, if there is a deadline, some action is
forced. If no action is taken, the deal is dead. The only way to
keep it alive is with action. (In real estate, if an offer is not
accepted by the deadline, it's automatically withdrawn.) When
there's a deadline, to procrastinate threatens the loss of the deal.
It now becomes preferable to take action.

From the buyer's perspective, setting a deadline may be the best
way to get the seller to act. The seller may outright accept the
offer, reject the offer, or make a counteroffer. In my experience,
most often the counteroffer is the result. Once the counteroffer
(with its own deadline for the buyer) is made, the negotiations can
move forward. Keep in mind that as counteroffers are made, both
parties are investing increasing amounts of time in the deal.

Trap

Just because you set deadlines, doesn't mean you'll always get
the deal you want. The deadline should be considered one tool
to be used in conjunction with many others. Beware of turning a
deadline into a "take it or leave it" threat. As we'll see shortly,
this tactic works less often than most people think.

RULE 20—Act Quickly

Once again, we're not in contradiction to the rule about investing time. Yes, you want the other party to invest time. But you
don't want to lose out to a better offer from someone else.

I can remember a broker friend working with buyers a few years ago, a very nice young couple, who wanted a home in a suburban area near San Francisco. Their problem, however, was that the Bay Area is very expensive, one of the most expensive in the United States. Homes in the neighborhood in which they were looking started at about $325,000 and went up in price from there. The most they could afford to pay, however, given the loan they could get and the down payment they had, was $300,000. They were, in effect, out of the market. But they were determined and they felt, correctly, that over time a desperate seller or two might pop up who would sell at a lower price.

It took several months, but the broker did find some sellers who wanted to get out immediately and were willing to accept a lower price to accomplish that. The sellers had already purchased another property. It was at the end of December, the worst season for selling a home, and they knew they had to compromise. They were asking $325,000 but indicated they would probably settle for $300,000—just barely within the buyers' range.

The trouble was that the buyers were finicky. They weren't sure about the room arrangement of the house. The kitchen seemed small, and the wife simply couldn't abide by the fact that there was no fireplace in the master bedroom. The broker agreed that these were, indeed, all problems with the property, but that because of their financial situation they had to compromise to get in. Further, sellers willing to settle for a low price were few and far between and unless the buyers acted quickly, they could lose out.

But the buyers weren't sure. They saw the house on Sunday, again the next Wednesday, and yet again the following weekend. But they couldn't make up their minds about making an offer. Finally, 2 weeks later they had talked it out and decided they could live with the property. They called the broker to say they would make a $300,000 offer. The broker, sadly, informed them that other buyers had offered the same amount and the seller had already agreed.

Needless to say, these buyers were unhappy and resolved to act more quickly in the future. Unfortunately, spring was coming, there were more buyers in the market, and they never did find another lower-priced house in that neighborhood.

Tip

Strike while the iron's hot. Real estate is a highly competitive field in all aspects. If you don't act quickly, someone else will and you could lose out on the deal.

Negotiating a deal can take place only when there are two parties. If you wait too long, the other party may already have negotiated a deal with someone else.

As a practical matter, when buying a home, jump in with both feet and learn everything about the market as fast as you can. Go out with brokers, visit homes for sale, check with realty boards, and familiarize yourself with what's out there and with what homes should cost. That way you'll recognize what you want when you see it and be able to act quickly. Remember, in a hot market where multiple offers are often made, you may have to act after seeing the property for only a few moments. Of course, in a slow market, you may have days or even weeks to act, but even then procrastination can let someone else sneak in and steal your deal.

Walking Away a Winner Is No Baloney

The gospel of negotiators has always been that a good deal means that both sides win. I get what I want and you get what you want.

However, this does not mean that each side comes away with what it wanted at the beginning or that one side doesn't come away with a lot more than the other. It means that the purpose of the negotiation is to get everything out on the table and to balance it all so that both parties can see what an equitable settlement is.

Sometimes, more often than not, one party will not even realize what it really wants or how strongly it wants it until negotiations are heated. Then, suddenly, the seller decides that she's got to have 90 days before moving and is willing to make concessions on price and terms to get it. Or the buyer decides he's got to have that second mortgage from the seller, even if it means paying more for the house.

Tip

Don't forget that you need to deal with People, Tactics, Strategy, and Time to get a win-win deal.

That's why it may appear to an outsider that one side comes away with more than another. In a truly successful negotiation, however, there is a just scale on which all things are balanced. And in the balance, it may appear to an onlooker as though one party got 90 percent and the other 10 percent. However, to the parties concerned, because of their strength of need or feeling, it is strictly a 50-50, win-win deal.

That's what negotiations are really all about. Find a way to give the other side what it wants so that you can get what you need.

5
Negotiating Price

Some of the most aggressive price negotiations I've ever seen in residential real estate have happened over the past few years in Southern California. Of course, it's important to understand that the Los Angeles area housing market has been severely depressed by a lingering regional recession fueled by massive job layoffs. As a result, real estate prices have plunged 30 percent or more in some areas. (But more recently have started recovering.) Nevertheless, many price negotiations have been truly remarkable.

For example, I have a friend who wanted to buy a home in the San Fernando Valley, just north of L.A. She found a house she liked in a fine neighborhood. The seller was asking $375,000, already reduced from $425,000. (You must remember that the L.A. and California markets are much higher than those in the rest of the country.)

At the time, prices were still soft and even declining a bit, so she felt that to be safe, she shouldn't offer more than $350,000. That way, she hoped, if prices continued to decline, they wouldn't drop below her acquisition cost. Of course, she was under no illusions that the seller would be anxious to accept such an offer. It would be very tough negotiating to get it accepted.

She was about to make this offer, when her mother reminded her that the market was depressed and had been so for several years. "Sellers are desperate to get out," her mother said. "Why not make a ridiculously low offer? Who knows? You might get it."

My friend considered the idea and then called several agents, who confirmed what her mother had said. She checked with articles in the local paper, which also confirmed that the market was just terrible. So she decided to give it a try. She had several alternative properties in mind, if she didn't get this one, and so was willing to take the risk. She offered $250,000, cash. (Cash meant she would put $25,000 down and get a loan for $225,000. It was cash to the seller.) She put up $5000 in an earnest money deposit. And she insisted on presenting the offer directly to the seller herself.

Needless to say, the seller was not pleased. He was, in fact, insulted by the offer and ranted and raved a bit. But my friend kept her cool and was pleasant, emphasizing that it was strictly a business proposition—nothing personal was involved. Eventually the seller calmed down and said that, of course, he could not accept such an offer. He owed $325,000 on the property. She was offering him $75,000 less than he owed!

My friend nodded calmly and sympathetically and then asked, "*Why* are you trying to sell in this market at all? Wouldn't it be better to wait until times improve."

The seller winced and admitted he had lost his job. He was 7 months behind in his mortgage payments and the lender was halfway through the foreclosure process, which takes a little over 3 months in California. He was desperate to sell. If my friend would just come up with enough money to cover the mortgage, the real estate commission, and closing costs—about $350,000—he would gladly give her the property for that price. That was just what she had hoped to buy the property for originally!

They talked into the early morning hours and developed a bond of trust. The seller, at this point, had just about given up any hope of getting any money for himself out of the property. What he wanted was some way to avoid foreclosure and the resulting ruination of his credit. My friend said she'd see what she could do.

The next day my friend contacted the lender, a local bank. With the seller's permission and aid, she finally talked to the person who was handling the foreclosure. He said the bank would be happy to cooperate and would even transfer the mortgage to my friend, if she would only take it at face value.

My friend thought this was an unusual proposition, since banks rarely transferred mortgages—almost never without jacking up the interest rate or at least without qualifying the new borrower. So she investigated further.

As it turned out, the bank itself was shaky, currently trying to fend off the Federal Deposit Insurance Corporation (FDIC) and federal officials, who were considering shutting it down because of insufficient capitalization caused by numerous other foreclosures on its books. This mortgage might be just the straw to break the camel's back. As a $325,000 loan, it showed up as an asset, even though currently nonperforming. But once the bank foreclosed, it would become an REO, or real-estate-owned property and it would move to the other side of the ledger. She figured—correctly as it turned out—that the bank was desperate to avoid any more foreclosures just then.

So she offered the bank $250,000 if it would sign off. Known as a *short payoff*, the deal meant that the seller would have to take nothing for his equity and the bank would have to accept a loss of $75,000. The bank officer immediately refused. So she pressed him, insisting that the officer present her offer to the bank committee responsible for REOs. He reluctantly did so. A few days later, he reported that they had listened to her offer with interest, but had turned it down. She said she would keep her offer open and asked the officer to return it that way to the committee. He agreed.

The seller also remained adamant against the offer, since after all he'd still be responsible for at least the agent's commission. Needless to say, the agent wasn't too anxious to complete this deal either.

So my friend let it sit. She called the seller weekly to ask about any other offers he had received (he received none) and to repeat her offer. She did the same to the bank officer. Time passed.

One Monday about 6 weeks later (it was just about the end of the time period for foreclosing on the property) she got a call from the bank officer. He said that if she came up with the $250,000 by week's end, the bank's committee had agreed to sign off. Of course, my friend had already arranged other financing, so this was no problem. There was, however, the seller to contend with.

She met the seller on Tuesday evening. They talked at length and she explained that this was a way of saving some of his credit. No foreclosure would go on his record, if he agreed. But, the seller countered, he still owed the agent a commission, $15,000 at the new sales price. And there were still some closing costs.

My friend said she would take care of the closing costs. But he would have to pay the agent's commission out of his pocket. The seller was aghast. He had no money. My friend suggested he offer the agent a promissory note.

The conclusion of this true story is that the bank, faced with taking back a property it couldn't swallow, agreed to the lesser evil of a $250,000 payoff of its $325,000 mortgage. The seller agreed to sign off the property receiving nothing from the sale. And the agent (there was only one broker involved), realizing that in a day or two the property would be lost to foreclosure and she would get nothing out of it anyway, agreed to taking back a promissory note that might be worth something in the future, when the seller got back on his feet with a new job.

My friend, of course, got a $250,000 house that as soon as the market turned around would be (and was) worth 50 percent more!

Did She Follow the Rules?

Keep in mind that this example observes many of the negotiating rules discussed in the previous chapters.

People

My friend never offended the seller, thus keeping the deal always negotiable. She dealt directly with the seller and the lender, who had the power to make decisions. She always was aboveboard in her offers, never doing anything sneaky.

Time

She got both the bank and the seller involved with her offer by constantly checking back with them. At the deal's conclusion, they both had a lot of time invested and ultimately part of their decision to move forward had to be because her offer was constantly before them. And when it counted (coming up with the $250,000), she was able to act quickly by previously making arrangements with another lender.

Tactics

Also, she asked "Why?" and got the answer that made the deal possible. She questioned authority—the loan officer who said the bank would never make such a deal. She listened carefully to learn how much the seller owed and what he was willing to do.

Planning

My friend had alternate properties in mind, so she wasn't committed totally to this deal. That allowed her to take big chances on the price. She also went to the trouble of being informed about the market and finding out who to talk to at the bank. She got the information necessary to make this deal. Finally, she worked only on those issues with could be resolved—namely, the bank's ability to accept less than the full amount for the mortgage. She didn't accept the pie analogy, but instead found a creative way for the agent to be paid, thus making the deal possible. And she didn't set a bottom line. Remember, her original bottom line was $350,000, fully $100,000 more than she ultimately paid for the property!

Will It Happen Every Time?

I was a bit hesitant to present the above example for fear that it would send the wrong message—namely, that you can negotiate any price down to any level at any time. That's simply not the case. In the harsh, cold light of reality, you *can* negotiate anything. But at some point you reach a level, particularly with price, at which the buyer or seller (or banker) can't or won't budge.

Think of it as loading a mule with bricks. If you ask the seller, for example, to come down $500 in price, you have loaded one heavy brick on the mule. If you ask the seller to come down $5000, it's 10 heavy bricks. Ask the seller to come down $10,000 and it's 20 heavy bricks—$20,000 and it's 40 heavy bricks.

You get the idea. The greater the price change you try to negotiate, the heavier the load. But eventually you'll get enough bricks on that mule to crush it. And that's as far down as the price will go.

Realistic negotiating recognizes limitations. (If you push too far, you kill the mule.)

How Much Should You Offer?

Often the price depends on factors totally outside the deal itself. Perhaps the most significant factor is the condition of the market at the time you're selling or buying. In our beginning example, the market was terrible; hence, a very low price was possible. It was largely market conditions that made this deal possible.

The Market Influence

Now consider the same example but suppose the market had been "hot." In a hot market, prices are appreciating and, as a result, there are a lot of buyers. My friend would never have been able to get such a good deal because in a hot market, someone else would have come in and bought the property long before the bank was in the final stages of foreclosure. Indeed, in a hot market the seller would have been able to sell long before foreclosure was even started, probably for a price closer to $400,000. What made the deal possible for my friend was that there were no other buyers; there was no real competition for the house.

Contrast this with a hot market in which a seller may get three or more offers for the property, often for more than the asking price, within days of listing it. Are you going to be able to negotiate that seller down in price in such a market? Hardly.

Determine Real Estate Market Conditions

Knowledge (see Rule 13) is the key to success here. Judging the market condition is the first step in determining how far you are able to negotiate a price. My suggestion is that before you even delve into the specifics of buying or selling a home, you do the following:

- Spend several mornings, particularly on Sundays, reading the real estate sections of several local newspapers. Find out what the columnists say about the market. Look at ads for repos (repossessed property) and auctions which indicate a bad market.

- Talk with at least three different agents, not about specific properties (although that will certainly come up) but about the market. How have sales been? How high is the inventory of houses in the multiple listing service? (Anything over 4 months is considered high and indicates a slow market.) Are sellers getting their prices, or are homes selling far below "asking"? Are multiple offers on homes a common occurrence? Or do houses sit for months and even years with no interest in them?

- Talk with at least one mortgage broker. Ask how many mortgages are being financed. Are the loans mostly refinances (owners taking new loans on existing homes), indicating a weak resale market? Or are there lots of loans on sale properties, indicating strong activity in the market?

It won't take you long to get a feel for the market in your area. Is it a "blowout," as was the case above in the Los Angeles area a few years ago? Is it a "hot" market, as is the case in parts of the Midwest as this book is written? Or is the market more sedate, with houses selling but no real price appreciation—in essence, a slow market?

Trap

Don't feel you can't sell in a bad market or can't buy in a hot market. You can, if you adjust your thinking to match the market conditions.

Respond to the Market

Once you determine just what the current market is in your area, you should prepare your negotiations accordingly. In a hot market if you're a buyer, be prepared to act quickly and also to pay close to full price or, in some instances, higher than full price in order to get a sale. Successfully negotiating price here may mean getting the house at only 1 percent *more* than the seller was asking! (If you had waited, you might have ended up paying 3 percent more as the market rapidly escalated upward.) If you're a seller, your plan of action may be to avoid negotiations altogether. Let the hot offers pile in; let the multiple buyers compete with one another.

In a cold market, the opposite is the case. As a buyer, you now have time on your side, as we've seen above. As a seller, you will want to act as quickly as possible, perhaps by lowering your price dramatically. A successful negotiation for a seller may mean getting out today at only a 4 percent loss instead of waiting 6 months and having to accept a 15 percent loss.

In a slow or average market, however, some real give-and-take can occur. As a buyer, you will be trying to convince the seller that the market is worse than it really is. As a seller, you will take the opposite approach. Here all the rules of negotiating we've discussed are likely to come into play.

Price Points

It's important to understand the concept of *price points* when considering your real estate market. It is easy to assume that because the market is down, no houses at any price level are selling. Or because the market is up, houses at all price levels are selling equally well.

That's not the way it usually works. Consider the L.A. regional market again. When the market was at its worst, houses were still selling in the "under $200,000" price range. Houses that were selling for around $150,000 actually did quite well. People still had to have a place to live and were willing to buy, as long as they felt the house couldn't go much lower in value.

In essence, at the worst of the market, if you had a house for $400,000, you probably couldn't get a single offer. But if you had a house for under $200,000, you could get many offers. (I know, because at the time I very quickly sold one in that market just below that price point.)

Similarly, when the market is hot and houses are moving up in value, often homes at the top end do very well while those at the bottom languish.

If you're buying (or selling), it's important to determine not only the overall market conditions, but the price points within that market. Maybe the market's doing badly, but you have a low-priced home at a price point that commands a lot of interest. You'll probably be less inclined to negotiate a much lower price. On the other hand, if you've got a high-priced home at a price point at which houses simply aren't moving, you're more likely to negotiate down.

Tip

I've found that good real estate agents are quite sensitive to these price points, although they may not identify them as such. The agent may say, "Homes priced between $80,000 and $100,000 are doing very well, but as soon as you go over $100,000, there's almost no activity. If several agents tell you this, you can probably put credence in their advice. They've just identified important price points for you.

Determine the Seller's Motivation

If you're a buyer, once you've determined the general condition of the market and how you will respond to it, your next goal (after identifying a property) is to determine the seller's motivation in selling. There can be 100 different reasons that a seller wants out of a property. The exact reason itself isn't important. What is important is how much pressure that reason puts on the seller.

As our example showed, a seller faced with a loss of income and foreclosure is going to be highly motivated. That seller will do almost anything, even pay out money (in our example, a note to the agent) to conclude a deal. On the other hand, a seller who is employed and who simply wants to move up to a larger home is likely to be less motivated. This seller may be far more willing to refuse to negotiate a lower price no matter what you say or offer. The motivation simply isn't there.

Tip

Real estate agents always emphasize motivation when they describe a seller. A "highly motivated" seller is one who has to get out. A seller who "lacks motivation" can simply sit on the property and wait for the right deal to come in. Smart buyers don't just look for a property; they also look for the highly motivated seller.

The really tricky part about motivation is determining what it is. Sometimes a seller who is highly motivated will instruct his or her agent to broadcast that fact as far and as loudly as possible: "Tell everybody I'm motivated. Bring in those deals!"

Maybe. But sometimes this is just a ploy to get buyers to make offers. The seller hopes that he or she can convert those lowball offers into higher prices through negotiation.

Trap

If you tell people you are highly motivated, you will get more offers. But the offers will be of lower quality, particularly the price. And you will have greater difficulty negotiating a higher price because the buyers you attract will tend to be only those looking for a "steal."

Determine the Demand for the Property

Not all peaches are created equally and neither are all properties. Ripe, round peaches with a fresh aroma and a perfect skin (no bruises) will command top dollar. Houses that are located in desirable neighborhoods, have a view or are close to an amenity such as a golf course or lake, and show well likewise command top dollar.

In other words, if you are buying a "bruised" property, you are more likely to be able to negotiate a lower price than if you are buying a property perfect in all aspects. This holds true regardless of the market conditions or the seller's motivation.

Trap

This rule of thumb does not mean that a great house in a great location will always sell for a great price. It just means that in any given market, such a house will always bring top dollar and will sell faster than a house in a lesser neighborhood that doesn't show nearly as well.

If you have spent some time looking at the market, you should be able to roughly determine the demand for any given house. Very quickly you will come to know which neighborhoods are more desirable and which are less. The seller or agent will immediately let you know about any special feature, such as a view or proximity to a golf course. And your own eyes will tell you if the house has terrific "curb appeal"—if it shows well to a buyer.

If you determine that the house you are buying (or selling) is a real peach, then for any given market you should expect more and better offers. If, on the other hand, the house needs paint and cleanup (or more serious rehabilitation), the neighborhood is a dump, and the property sticks right out on a corner lot by two heavily traveled streets, then expect fewer offers (buying or selling) at lower prices.

The Bottom Line

Ultimately what you probably want to know is twofold. How much less should you offer for a house? And how far down (or up) can you negotiate the price?

Unfortunately, there are no set rules here. Some gurus I have read say, "Always offer 5 percent lower than what the seller is asking." Maybe. But in a hot market in which sellers are getting full price or more, you're just wasting everyone's time and may miss out on a good deal.

My suggestion is that you observe the following guidelines both for the offer and for negotiating the price up or down after the offer:

Guide to Negotiating Price

Offer More

Less Negotiating Room

↑   Hot Market

| Unmotivated Seller

| Good Price Point

| Great Neighborhood and Location

| Home in Terrific Condition

|

|

|

| Home in Terrible Condition

| Lousy Neighborhood and Location

| Bad Price Point

| Highly Motivated Seller

| Stone Cold (Blowout) Market

↓

More Negotiating Room

Offer Less

6
Negotiating the Real Estate Commission

I have a good friend who to this day is fond of recalling the first time he ever listed a house with an agent.

"She came in, we talked a little while, and then she said she wanted a 7 percent commission. I was flabbergasted. I knew that other agents in the area were charging only 5 percent. She was 2 percent higher.

"When I began to protest, she wiggled her finger at me and said, 'You've got a miserable little house in a crime-ridden neighborhood. You should be glad I'm willing to list it at all!'"

There's usually a pause in the story at this point where I'm supposed to ask, "So what did you do?" He's a good friend, so I usually go along.

"Why, I threw her out! I told her I didn't need to sell. We lived there another 5 years and then I sold it myself for twice what we paid! Now that's getting a good deal."

I suppose this story is supposed to have several morals, one, according to my friend, is that agents are greedy know-nothings and another, that he is a real wheeler and dealer. The truth of the matter, however, is that I knew him when he lived in that house and it indeed was small and miserable and in a terrible neighborhood. I can understand why an agent would want a bigger commission to sell it.

Further, because he didn't list, he had to live there another 5 years until all real estate took a big hike in price (around 1978 in his area) and any fool could have gotten twice the purchase price of 10 years earlier.

My own moral here is that negotiating the real estate commission with the agent doesn't necessarily mean you will want to lower it. You may want to raise it to get a quicker sale!

Trap

Beware of any agent who says that the "fixed" or "standard" or "regular" commission is a given amount. In all parts of the country, the rate of commission paid to a licensed agent to list your house is entirely negotiable between you and the agent. There is no set rate. It's whatever the two of you agree upon.

Will You Get What You Pay For?

At the onset, it's important to keep track of what you want out of listing your house with an agent. While, of course, you want to pay as little as you can, on the other hand you also want to sell your property as soon as possible. It's sort of like watching the donut and not the hole. What's really important is selling the property. The agent's fee is or should be subordinate to that, not the other way around.

Therefore, when you sit down with an agent to negotiate the fee, you should also be negotiating the service. One is dependent on the other. If you want a lower fee, perhaps you'll have to expect lesser service. On the other hand, if you get super service, you may need to pay a higher fee. You usually get what you pay for.

How Does the Agent See It?

I think it's important to understand how agents see things. You might say this falls under the category of Rule 13 (Be informed) and Rule 9 (Question authority). If you don't know what the agent has to do to sell your house, you can't really talk price with him or her. You may have unrealistic expectations.

Despite what most people think, real estate agents are not highly paid. Most agents, even active ones, make less than $40,000 a year. (Of course, there are always a few who make a million, but that really is the exception.)

Most active agents (as opposed to those who work part time and don't really do much in the field) are on the job 50 or 60 hours a week, including nights and weekends. They answer calls at all hours, often from their homes, and drive people whom they've often just met into all sorts of neighborhoods. Even when they finish the job and get a sale, they may be threatened with a lawsuit by an angry buyer or seller for something they (or chances are someone else) overlooked.

Further, they must pay for their own clothes (agents have to dress nicely), their own car (including gas, maintenance, and insurance), and sometimes even their own office space and advertising. And on most deals they finally make, they must split the commission between a listing and selling office. If the agent is only a salesperson, the commission must be further split between the salesperson and the broker. (And there's no salary—no deal, no income.)

No, I'm not an apologist for agents. It's just that I've been there and I know what it's like. To simply say that an agent, a good one, doesn't earn his or her commission is poppycock. To a seller, the agent's work and expenses may not always be obvious. But rest assured a lot of work and expense go into selling properties.

How Does the Seller See It?

I'm sure you're familiar with this perspective. You've got a house worth $200,000. You want to sell it and an agent waltzes in and asks for a 6 percent commission, a full $12,000. Chances are you owe $150,000 on the house, so the agent is asking for nearly a quarter of your $50,000 equity, just to find a buyer! (If you owe more, the agent's percentage of your equity is going to be even higher.)

It's unconscionable, you say. However, what are your choices? You could always sell the property yourself, if you have the time, the patience, and the know-how. Few people do, however.

So now it becomes a matter of negotiating the agent's fee downward. The agent wants 6 percent; you want to pay 1 percent. The agent wants to get a full commission, because of his or her expenses, time, and so on. Your hope is to get the fee knocked down so you won't be "throwing away" so much of your equity. The result, of course, is negotiation.

Trap

When you're negotiating with an agent, remember that the agent's choices are limited too. The agent has a choice of listing your property at whatever rate he or she can get. Or walking away. If agents walk, their time spent on you is wasted. A few agents, therefore, will ultimately accept any commission rate and then do nothing to sell the property. Their rationale is the following: If by chance it sells, they get something. If it doesn't, they haven't invested any more of their time. You want to avoid this sort of arrangement like the plague.

How Are Buyers Found?

Before we proceed, it's worthwhile to take a quick look at how agents actually find buyers. It's really nothing more than a game of numbers.

When you put your house up for sale, you can pretty much know that somewhere out there is a buyer. The hard part is winnowing out all the noninterested lookers and getting that one who will purchase your property to look at it and say yes.

Time is an important part of this game. The more actively you look for that right buyer, the less time it will take to sell. On the other hand, if you don't spend very much time looking, chances are your property will "age," in the parlance of agents. It will sit there without anyone coming to look at it. For practical purposes, when no one comes to see your house, you might as well not have it up for sale. I've seen properties that just have a sign placed out front. No active sales effort is made. The owners have sat for years waiting for Mr. and Mrs. Right Buyer to come by. Some of these houses never sell, with the discouraged sellers simply withdrawing from the market.

Yes, you can look for buyers yourself. But the fact is that 80 to 90 percent of all residential real estate in most areas is sold through agents. When buyers want to see properties, they contact an agent. When sellers want to sell, they list with an agent.

Tip

Think what this really means. At any given time in any given area, roughly 80 to 90 percent of *all* current buyers and sellers are in contact with agents.

Therefore, operating on the premise that it's futile to reinvent the wheel, it's usually not worthwhile for you to try to contact these potential buyers directly when agents are already in contact with them; your best chance of selling is through the agents who are already working with buyers.

What Role Does the Agent Play?

What does an agent do for you? A good active real estate agent who makes a concerted effort to sell your property will do the following: Besides the obvious sales tools such as placing advertising in newspapers, holding open houses, putting a sign on the property, and setting up a "lockbox" so other agents can show it, your broker will also "talk up" your house at sales meetings. Large brokerage firms have at least one sales meeting a week which all agents attend.

If your agent "co-brokes" the property (shares the listing with other brokers and, accordingly, splits the commission), he or she should attend MLS (multiple listing services) meetings at least twice a month. Here, agents from all the real estate companies in the area gather. Your agent can stand up at these meetings and tell other agents from dozens of other offices about this wonderful property (yours), its features, low price, good terms, and so on. If your agent attends enough of these meetings and talks up your property to enough other agents, chances are one of them will be working with that buyer who could be just right for your property.

A few agents won't want to co-broke your home. They'll tell you they have a better chance of selling if they list only for their office. (They'll advertise it more, show it more, and so on.) This is nonsense. You want the maximum number of *agents* made aware of and working on your house. If a broker insists on not co-broking a property, I'd wonder if he or she was just trying to avoid splitting a commission.

In other words, the most effective thing your agent can do is "talk up" your house to as many other agents as possible. Since agents in the area are in contact with the vast majority of buyers, co-broking immediately increases your chances that the right buyer will hear about your home.

Open House

It's a mistake to think that an "open house" primarily benefits the seller of the house that's held open. Studies have repeatedly shown that potential buyers almost never purchase a home that they come to visit under these circumstances. Rather, the agent on duty tries to convert these buyers to clients by finding what they're really looking for and then showing them other properties. In some areas, it has even been considered unethical conduct for an agent to tell sellers that an "open house" will help sell their property.

On the other hand, a lot of agents holding open houses elsewhere may stumble across a potential buyer for yours and bring that buyer by, even though your house isn't open. In a reciprocal sort of way, therefore, "open houses" do help sellers.

What's the True Role of the Commission?

Consider that you negotiate a reduced commission. Now your agent stands up before other agents at a large sales meeting and describes how nice your four-bedroom, three-bath house shows to buyers. A colleague raises a hand and asks, "What's the commission rate?"

Your agent replies, "Four percent."

If there are a lot of houses listed at 5, 6, and even 7 percent, all else being equal, whose houses do you think agents are inclined to show their clients first?

Tip

Agents are required to show buyers all properties that are appropriate for them, without regard to what commission rate the agents might make. That's part of their fiduciary relationship. In the real world, however, where judgment is a big factor, that's not the way things always work out.

On the other hand, let's say that you have negotiated something quite different. You have told your agent you're willing to pay a 6 percent commission, which happens to be what's commonly paid in your area at the time.

Further, you say you're offering an all-expense-paid week in Hawaii to the selling agent who brings in a buyer. Now your agent stands up at one of these crucial meetings and describes your house. When someone asks what the commission rate is, your broker beams and says, "My client will not only pay a 6 percent commission, she will also give an all-expense-paid week in Hawaii to the selling agent!" You should be able to hear the cheers.

Now, when another agent has a prospective buyer, all things being equal, which house do you think that buyer likely will see first?

Tip

Rather than increasing the rate of the commission, offer bonuses to agents who sell quickly or who sell at all. Trips, television sets, even an old car or boat that you own and want to get rid of can be offered. As long as the item is tangible (not money), it has the potential of capturing the imagination of other agents and helps make your property stand out. Also, most such bonuses are actually cheaper than offering a higher commission.

How Do You Negotiate for the Agent's Services?

When you negotiate with an agent over a listing, keep upper-most in your mind the service the agent is going to perform. How will the agent promote your home? You should be concerned with these questions:

- Will the agent "talk up" your home at sales meetings? How many? How often? To how many agents?

- Will your agent co-broke the property with other agents in the area? Will he or she list your property on the multiple listing service?

- What plusses can the agent find to help induce other agents to bring buyers to your house?

- How much advertising will the listing agency do as a whole? It's not necessary just to advertise your specific home to find a buyer for it. Large amounts of advertising bring in lots of buyers, one of whom may be just right.

- Does your agent have other sources of potential buyers? For example, does the listing office have contacts with other offices nationwide that might refer transferees to your area?

In other words, what you should really be negotiating about is what the agent will do to promote the sale of your property, especially how he or she will talk it up to other agents. Only when you've reached a satisfactory arrangement for services should you negotiate price.

How Do You Negotiate for the Agent's Fee?

All agents will (or should) tell you up front that the listing fee is negotiable. However, they may also say something like this: "Even though the fee is negotiable, our office accepts only listings for 6 percent." Or, "Our bottom line is no less than 5 percent." The agent can legitimately turn down a listing if he or she feels the commission rate is too low.

A truly candid agent may also tell you that currently nearly all houses in your area are listed at, for example, 6 percent. If you list for 5 percent, you will be offering 1 percent below the market. If you list for 3 percent, you'll be offering half of what most other sellers will pay. And your agent may point out the disadvantages to you of doing this, as noted above.

On the other hand, you can point out other factors. For example, if the market is strong, it doesn't take a whole lot of effort to sell a home. It wasn't so long ago that buyers were plentiful (and still are in some areas) and frequently bid against one another for each house as it was listed.

In a situation where properties are selling almost as fast as listed, it's silly to pay a full commission. Since the market is so hot, it won't really make much difference (perhaps a few weeks) whether you offer the agent 6 percent or 3 percent. As soon as a sign goes up, buyers will come by.

Further, in a hot market, listing rates tend to fall. You're not the only one who realizes that paying the full rate is foolish. Other sellers do as well and that puts downward pressure on the market. Agents may still try to get a higher listing commission rate, but savvy buyers won't let them. Besides, in such a market, sales are so plentiful that almost any agent should do well regardless of the listing rate.

On the other hand, in a very slow market, attempting to cut the commission rate would probably work against you. If you are serious about selling, you will want to get out of your property as quickly as possible, before the value drops further. That means getting as many agents as possible working for you, and a high commission rate can help. I have seen sellers negotiate a 7 percent commission when 6 percent was common, as long as the agent promised quick action by talking up the property.

Tip

Remember, time is money. The more time you spend trying to sell your property, the more money you'll spend on that property.

Should You Deal with Discount Brokers?

There are agents out there who regularly work for less. Help-U-Sell and other national agencies have a sliding scale of commission rates that depend on just how much work you do as part of the selling. If you show the house and pay for the advertising, you might get a 4 percent rate, for example. For just handling the paperwork, some brokers will simply charge a flat fee, say one or two thousand dollars. On the other hand, if you want full service, you might end up paying 6 or 7 percent.

Does it pay to deal with discount real estate companies? My own experience is that you get what you pay for. Discount brokers today list their homes on multiple listing services right along with full-service brokers. Their commission rate also is usually given on every listing.

As noted, in a hot market it is probably foolish to list for a high rate, since your house is likely to sell no matter how much or how little effort is poured into it. In a cold market, however, you need all the help you can get.

Tip

In a really hot market, you can save the entire commission by selling "by owner." If you have enough experience, you can do it yourself.

Trap

In a cold or blown-out market, it may be difficult to sell by owner. There are so few buyers that you may need the services of an agent to complete a sale.

What About Negotiating the Commission as a Percentage of Equity?

At various times in the past I've seen ideas put forth that would change the listing system in real estate. Instead of the listing commission being a percentage of the sales price, it would be a percentage of the equity.

For example, you have a house that sells for $100,000 and you list at a 6 percent commission. The agent receives $6000.

On the other hand, you have only $15,000 in equity in your property; the rest is mortgaged. If the agent's fees were based on equity, at 6 percent the agent would receive only $900.

I know that sellers will be enthusiastic about this sort of arrangement, but any good real estate agent will explain that it simply won't work. No agent can afford to work for that kind of commission.

Further, agents will argue, your equity really shouldn't be the basis of the commission. After all, the price and the mortgageable amount are based not on seller's equity, but on what the house is worth on the open market. Why should the commission be different? Besides, the buyer's agent is paid a commission on the basis of sales price, not seller's equity. Finally, for any given price, there are bound to be hundreds of sellers, each with a different equity. Thus, a commission system based on equity simply would be unworkable.

In short, I wouldn't hold out much hope for an equity-based system of commission rates to be enacted by any real estate company any time soon.

Can You Get the Agent to Accept Paper Instead of Cash?

In our opening example, the agent accepted paper (a promissory note) instead of cash. That, in fact, was part of the negotiations.

However, when you sign a listing, all agents will insist on cash. In fact, they will want it written into the listing agreement that you owe them a cash commission if they produce a buyer "ready, willing, and able" to purchase, even if you back out of the sale!

Trap

The agent is technically entitled to a commission not when the sale closes, but when he or she produces an appropriate buyer.

It's something to consider before listing if you're not fully convinced you want to sell.

Tip

It's not necessary that you ask an agent to take cash *or* paper. You could negotiate a split: some cash and the rest paper. There can be any combination of the two, depending on how you negotiate the deal.

Some agents are adamant and will not cut their commission or accept anything but cash, no matter what. Other agents, however, are willing to compromise on their commission if they see no other way to make this deal and only a remote possibility of other deals coming up on the property.

However, even if your agent is willing to take paper or cut a commission, be aware that others agents are probably involved. If there are two agents in on the deal, a buyer's agent and a seller's agent, both would have to agree on taking paper or on reducing the commission. Further, you may be dealing with salespeople instead of brokers. Thus, before they can give you the go-ahead, they may have to get their broker's permission. And while the salesperson may be eager to make even a reduced commission on a sale, the broker may nix the idea on principle or policy—the agency simply doesn't do that sort of thing.

All this is negotiable. The trouble is that when it comes to a commission, so many people can get involved that the negotiations over the commission can be more extensive and heated than those over the sale!

Tip

If you are going to negotiate the sales commission lower or include paper instead of cash, usually the best time to do so is when you've got a deal in hand whose success or failure hinges on how the commission is handled. It's far harder for the agent to say no then. Unfortunately, it may also be far harder for you to say no, too.

The Bottom Line

Keep in mind that getting the best deal doesn't necessarily mean getting the lowest commission rate. If what you want is a quick sale in a slow market, successful negotiating may mean giving the agent more than he or she is asking for!

7

Negotiating a More Favorable Sales Agreement

I received a call not long ago from a friend who is now selling real estate after having been laid off from a long career with a high-tech engineering company. He's obviously new to this field and was having trouble with a sale.

"It's falling apart," he said. "I represent the sellers and we received a good offer from a buyer who put up a $5000 deposit and was paying 20 percent down in cash with an 80 percent loan. Everything seemed 'go.' The property was scheduled to close last Thursday, then at the last minute, we learned that the lender refused to fund the mortgage. The bank said there was some problem with the buyer's credit. Apparently the buyer didn't tell us, but she's been shopping around for a loan for over 2 months and hasn't found one yet. What do I do now?"

Looking to the ceiling, I was about to suggest an appeal to a higher authority, but demurred. Instead, I suggested that my friend find out what the credit problem was by attempting to contact the buyer's agent, the buyer, or the lender and by offering aid in any way he could. At the same time, I suggested he immediately put the house back on the market.

My friend said the seller had agreed to a 120-day escrow (exceedingly long for a residential sale), with 50 days to go. He couldn't very well put the house back on the market yet. "Prayer," I finally suggested aloud. "Try it."

The immediate problem here was that my friend had a wobbly (financially speaking) buyer. But the long-term problem was a badly negotiated sales agreement.

If my friend had been in real estate longer, he might have written into the sales agreement a contingency that the buyer had to produce a firm letter of commitment from a lender within 2 weeks—or else there was no deal. Although that wouldn't actually guarantee that the lender would fund the money, it would be a strong assurance of the fact. If there was a credit problem, a lender undoubtedly wouldn't have written such a letter. The seller would have learned of the credit problem within a couple of weeks and could have backed out of the deal gracefully, returning the house to the market. Only 2 weeks lost selling time, at most.

Also, the seller should have insisted that the time for closing the deal be much shorter, perhaps 60 days or less. Barring a contingency about lender's approval, now, after 70 days had passed, the buyer's chance to close would have passed and the seller could put the house back on the market.

"At least we can keep the deposit," my friend said. (When a buyer loses a deposit it is frequently split between seller and agent.) I told my friend that, sadly, that was most unlikely. Most sales agreements specifically state that if the buyer can't get financing, there's no deal and the deposit is to be returned.

I heard a long "Ohh" on the other end of the line. My friend definitely did not like that answer.

What Should You Look for in a Sales Agreement?

At the onset it's important to understand that the making of a real estate deal does not occur with the sales agreement document. It occurs in the understanding between buyer and seller. The sales agreement should only reflect that understanding.

However, the document itself is important, not only because it can be legally binding but because it often guides where the parties are heading.

The key to negotiating a more favorable sales agreement usually lies not in the boilerplate that comes with the standard form, but in the clauses you add—in other words, the specific terms and conditions, or contingencies, of the sale. Depending on these, you can have a better or worse deal and sales agreement.

In this chapter we're going to consider six negotiable areas:

- Price versus terms
- The deposit
- Financing
- Time
- Contingencies
- The buyer's final approval or walk-through

Tip

A contingency (or "subject to" statement) is an action that must be performed before the sale can go through. "This sale is *subject to* my Aunt Hilda's written approval of the property within 3 days" is an example.

Some 30 years ago, when I began in real estate, the sales agreement (then called the deposit receipt) was a single-page document with maybe a dozen preprinted lines (referring to such things as "time is the essence of the agreement"). Everything was filled in by the agent, buyer, or seller.

Litigation, however, has made the days of the handwritten sales agreement almost a thing of the past. Too many of the old documents simply didn't stand up in court because of vague or improper language. Today's agreement is quite different, often a half-dozen pages long, all filled with legal boilerplate. In some sales agreements there is room to write in only the address, the price, the down payment, and the loan amount. *Everything* else, including a long list of contingency clauses, is preprinted and written by lawyers. If you want one of the clauses to apply, you simply check the box and all parties initial! (Unfortunately, no agreement can anticipate every possible contingency a buyer or seller may want.)

Trap

The point, however, is that although buyer and seller may agree to contingencies, or unusual terms and conditions, in order to add these to a modern sales agreement, you may need the services of a lawyer or a very competent real estate agent. Unless you are extremely well versed in real estate, don't attempt adding to or changing a sales agreement yourself.

Should You Go for a Better Price or Better Terms?

Some agents think of the sales agreement as having two major parts. The first part is simply the price, the amount to be paid for the property. It occupies only a single line on the document.

The second part refers to the terms by which the price will be paid and how title will be given. Virtually all the remainder of the document comes under this heading.

The two-part breakdown, however, underscores the relationship between price and terms. In any real estate deal there is usually a trade-off between price and terms. For example, if the buyer is paying all cash within 2 weeks (or as soon as clear title can be given), you would naturally expect that the price would be lower than if the buyer is putting down no cash, but instead is borrowing money from a lender, the seller, and everyone else. In other words, typically the lesser the terms, the higher the price; the better the terms, the lower the price.

When negotiating the sales agreement (in essence negotiating the deal), therefore, always remember the two parts: price and terms. Give on one, get on the other. (This does not mean that you cannot increase the size of the pie or the total package, as noted in earlier chapters. It just means that within the sales agreement, a useful division is into the two parts.)

Hung Up on Price

Sometimes one party or the other will get hung up on price. Typically the seller becomes convinced that the only way to cut a good deal is to get his price.

If the buyer is savvy, she will go along with the price, but instead insist on trading off extremely favorable terms, to her. As a result, while the seller gets the price he wanted, he may actually be giving up so much in the terms of the deal that he ends up losing!

Trap

Beware of hanging onto price like a lifeboat. It could end up sinking you.

For the remainder of this chapter we're going to look into some of the terms and conditions that you may want to include in your sales agreement.

Should You Put Up a Deposit?

Buyer and seller do not usually negotiate on the deposit (although negotiations on increasing the deposit can occur, as we'll see shortly). Nevertheless, the deposit is a part of the negotiations, since it indicates the depth of the buyer's sincerity in making the deal.

The actual purpose of the deposit is to show that the buyer is sincere—hence, the correct term is *Earnest money deposit*. There is no reason a deal cannot be completed without a deposit. However, a buyer who does not put up a deposit is suggesting that he or she has little financial commitment to the purchase. A seller is far less inclined to look favorably on an offer without a deposit.

Trap

If you're a buyer, be sure that in any sales agreement you sign the clause stating that the deposit is to be used as part of the down payment as specified; otherwise it could be interpreted to be *in addition* to the down payment!

From the seller's perspective, presumably, the buyer is putting up money that will be lost if that buyer fails to complete the purchase. It's money at risk. Hence, if the buyer puts up $10,000, it presumably shows that the buyer is quite enthusiastic about the property and committed to the purchase.

Who Gets the Deposit?

That's the theory. The practice, however, is somewhat different. It has to do with how things work out with a deposit in the real world. The fact of the matter is that today buyers rarely lose their deposits in real estate, even when the sale doesn't go through entirely because it's their fault.

Assume that Sally wants to buy a home and puts up a $5000 deposit. As soon as the seller, John, accepts the offer, he is entitled to that money. It should be paid directly to him. Later, if the deal doesn't go through on John's part, it's up to Sally to get the deposit back from John. However, if John isn't entirely scrupulous or is just not very good at handling money, he may not want or be able to pay Sally back. Sally's recourse is to go to court and sue John for the recovery. The trouble is, of course, that the suit could cost more than the amount of the deposit to be recovered!

As you can see, this could be a messy business. It's a poor way to handle a deposit. Further, if an agent were involved, chances are that both Sally and John would blame that poor soul for what happened in the deal and insist that the agent come up with money.

More than anyone else, agents who are involved with deposits on a day-to-day basis realize the problems and potential pitfalls involved with giving the deposit to the seller.

Therefore, most suggest that the buyer make the deposit out to a third party. One choice is the agent, who can then keep it in a trust account. The trouble is that if the agent is the fiduciary of the seller and the seller insists on getting the deposit, the agent may have to turn it over—and then answer to the buyer about where the money went. This puts the agent in an even worse position.

Therefore, today most agents insist that the buyer make the deposit check to an escrow company. If the offer is accepted, the check is immediately deposited into escrow and there it sits until the deal is concluded—or later.

The "Or Later" Problem

If the deal isn't concluded for any reason, that deposit continues to sit in the escrow account. The buyer can't get it back unless the seller signs off. The seller can't get it unless the buyer signs off.

In actual practice, however, the seller may have difficulty in reselling to someone else while a deposit check from a previous buyer in escrow is outstanding, so the seller may sign off simply to be done with the old deal. As a result, in many cases the buyer gets the deposit back, sooner or later, no matter what. Rarely does the seller get to keep the deposit.

Trap

Buyer or seller can go to court and sue the other party to get that deposit check released out of escrow. But in residential real estate, the deposits are usually too small to warrant such expensive action. It's simpler to just settle.

A settlement over who gets the deposit when a deal goes sour is negotiable. Most often, the buyer gets it all back (real estate agents prefer such a practice because it tends to help their reputation and avoid malpractice lawsuits against them). But this doesn't have to be the case. The seller could get the entire deposit, or it could be split.

Sometimes a clever buyer will include a clause in the agreement that if the deal isn't concluded within 120 days for whatever reason, any deposit placed in escrow automatically reverts to the buyer. The seller will often agree, thinking that the intent of this clause is to encourage the seller to move the deal along. What the clause may really mean, however, is that all the buyer has to do is procrastinate to get that deposit back. Savvy sellers often will balk at such a contingency.

Failure to Complete the Transaction

Thus far our assumption has been that the deposit is all that's at stake. However, if a buyer fails to go through with a deal without having a valid reason for backing out, the seller can come back at the buyer for failure to complete the deal according to the sales agreement.

The Deposit as Liquidated Damages

This is a real risk for buyers and particularly for agents who usually get thrust into the middle of such angry actions. Therefore, today many agents include in their sales agreements a clause which specifies that in the event the buyer does not go through with the sale and has no legitimate reason for backing out, the deposit is automatically to be considered liquidated damages. In other words, the seller gets the money, but cannot sue for additional damages.

As a buyer, you have the option of agreeing or not with this condition. The plus is you don't have to worry about an angry seller suing you. (Yes, it's rare, but it could happen.) The minus is that you could really lose your deposit money! It's something to think about.

What Is the True Effect of the Deposit?

In residential real estate today, the deposit has the same function it always had: to demonstrate how sincere the buyer is. However, what it really means is that the buyer is willing to tie up a set amount of money for a potentially very long period of time. Any anticipation by the seller that he or she is going to be getting that money any time soon without a sale may be more wishful thinking than anything else.

How Big a Deposit Should You Offer?

As far as most sellers are concerned, the bigger the deposit the better. However, after a certain point additional amounts of money aren't going to tilt anyone's head. Remember, any realistic seller today knows that the chances of ever getting to that deposit if the deal sours may be remote.

Thus, the deposit amount should be large enough to show a commitment on the part of the buyer, but need not be overly large. My own feeling is that in today's economy an adequate deposit is $2000 on properties worth up to $100,000, perhaps $3500 on properties worth $150,000, and $5000 on properties above that. A larger deposit on very expensive properties may be appropriate.

These amounts show the seller a commitment to the deal, but do not tie up an unnecessarily large amount of the buyer's money.

Trap

Sometimes a buyer who has a particularly poor offer will submit a very large deposit. The hope is that the seller will focus on the deposit and not on the deal. Very few sellers are so naive today.

Sometimes savvy sellers can use the deposit to help ensure that the buyer will complete the transaction. For example, the buyer may offer a $5000 deposit. The seller may agree to the amount, but may stipulate that after all the contingencies (if any) in the agreement are met, the buyer will increase the deposit to $20,000.

Now there's quite a bit of difference between a $5000 deposit and a $20,000 one. Further, once all the contingencies in a deal are met, it is much more difficult for the buyer to find a loophole by which to get out of the deal. This means that the chances increase of the deposit getting hung up in escrow indefinitely or of the seller ultimately getting the deposit in case the buyer doesn't go through. Thus, such a condition helps ensure that the buyer will ultimately go through with the purchase.

On the other hand, if the buyer refuses to go along, the seller may question the buyer's sincerity and not sign the sales agreement. After all, why should a buyer who plans to make the purchase anyway hesitate in increasing the deposit once all the contingencies are met?

How Should the Financing Be Handled?

As we saw in the opening example, negotiating strict time limit contingencies on the buyer for obtaining needed financing should help protect the seller. These days sellers are always concerned (with some good reason) about buyers who talk a good deal but later can't come up with the money.

A buyer can sometimes use this seller's concern over financing to negotiate a better deal. If you're a buyer, why not go to a mortgage broker, bank, or savings and loan and get prequalified? Usually the only charge is the cost of a three-bureau credit report. (The three leading credit-reporting agencies are TransUnion, Equifax, and TRW. The report covers all three.) Now when you, the buyer, show up with an offer, you can plunk down a written commitment from a lender for a mortgage up to a set amount of money. The seller instantly knows that you'll qualify and that the loan's available (assuming, of course, that the house appraises for enough).

Tip

Armed with such a qualifying letter, you can edge out other less qualified offers in a hot market. In a slow market, you may be able to leverage the letter into a lower price or better terms.

Beyond the matter of whether the buyer can get a mortgage is how the financing is to be handled. In the simplest of deals, the buyer will offer 20 percent down to an 80 percent loan at the market interest rate for 30 years.

A wise seller will not include in the sales agreement the exact interest rate and payment that the buyer is to qualify for. The reason is that interest rates tend to bob around. If the market rate is 7 percent when you sign the agreement and you write that in, but it jumps to 8 percent by the time the deal is ready to close, you've given the buyer a way to back out—he or she can no longer get a 7 percent mortgage.

The wise buyer wants to be protected from having to go through with a purchase for a higher interest rate (and, accordingly, a higher monthly payment) than he or she feels comfortable paying. Therefore, even though the seller may not want to lock in the current interest rate in the sales agreement, the buyer may insist on locking in an interest rate.

One way to negotiate a win-win situation for both buyer and seller is to put in a maximum interest rate and payment that the buyer will accept. Say that rates are currently 7 percent. Perhaps the agreement could call for a loan for "not more than 7.5 percent interest." This limits the buyer's risk should rates rise and also gives some assurance to the seller that the buyer isn't going to use a financing contingency to escape from the deal.

As further protection, the buyer may want to insist that the exact term and type of loan also be written in as a contingency. For example, the sale may be contingent upon the buyer applying for and obtaining a fixed rate mortgage for 30 years with payments of no more than $1100 per month and an annual interest rate of no more than 9 percent. If it's an adjustable rate mortgage (ARM), that fact should also be written in, along with the minimum steps, adjustment periods, margins, and so forth. (More information on ARMs is available in my book *Tips and Traps When Mortgage Hunting*, McGraw-Hill, 1992.)

Negotiating Finance Terms

An "80/20" deal (80 percent financing, 20 percent down) usually means cash to the seller, but it may not always be what a buyer wants. As a buyer, you may want to put less money down—for example, a 10 percent or even 5 percent down payment. While there are institutional lenders (banks, S&Ls, insurance companies, and so on) that do handle 90 percent or even 95 percent mortgages, these loans are more difficult to find and to qualify for. As a result, you may want to have the seller help you with the financing in the form of a second mortgage.

Sometimes sellers want to finance their properties, especially when the homes are paid off and the sellers are retirees. They may like the idea of having their regular income earn a higher rate than the savings account or CD that a mortgage provides. If a seller handles all the financing, there usually are far fewer problems with qualifying. This means that a seller with financing may be able to negotiate a better price and other terms from a needy buyer.

Most sellers, however, want only cash. Maybe they need the money to invest in another home. Maybe they're simply scared of giving credit to a buyer. Maybe they just don't want the bother.

In any event, this becomes a deal point. You the buyer want the seller to handle the financing. But the seller doesn't want to do that. How do you negotiate the point?

There are a variety of solutions. Sometimes the seller can be induced to carry back a second mortgage that he or she doesn't want by getting a higher price on the sale, by getting a higher interest rate, or by gaining concessions on time or other conditions in the deal. In other words, if you're the buyer who needs to have a reluctant seller carry back a second mortgage, it may be to your advantage to negotiate a higher price or better terms elsewhere. Again, this will produce a win-win situation. You get what you want (seller financing) by finding something the seller wants.

A few years ago unscrupulous speculators abused the financing deal point by pushing it too far. They asked sellers to carry 100 percent of the financing. In other words, they offered nothing down. They would buy "subject to" the existing first mortgage (meaning they didn't assume liability for it) and the seller would give them a second mortgage for the entire balance.

To get sellers to agree, the buyers jacked up the price often beyond market value. Their plan usually was twofold: (1) to get hold of the property, rent it out, and wait for rapid price appreciation to overtake them and then (2) to sell for a profit, having invested next to nothing. Or the more unscrupulous, having gotten control, would violate the property. They rented it, kept the rental money, and made no payments to the lender (of the first mortgage) or to the seller (who held the second). By the time foreclosure was completed, they often had up to a year of rent that they pocketed. The person who got hurt was the seller, who was still responsible for the existing first mortgage and who received no payment on the second. Some sellers simply lost their properties and their equities. Others got their properties back, but at great expense.

Trap

If you're a seller, beware of a buyer who wants you to carry back any financing. My advice is never to accept less than 10 percent down and be sure to check the buyer's credit carefully. Never allow the buyer 100 percent financing, no matter what price you may be offered. Remember, if a deals sounds too good to be true, it usually is.

How Do You Deal with Time?

Time can also be a deal point. In Chapter 4, we saw why time was important as a negotiating tool. Now we'll consider a specific application of time in the sales agreement: the date of occupancy.

When (the exact date) the seller turns the home over to the buyer is usually a point of vital interest to both parties. Normally, occupancy is given to the buyer on the date the house transfers title. But there are exceptions. For example, a few years ago I was selling a house and the buyers, as part of the sales offer, wanted to be in the property within 30 days. The buyers were coming from Central America and their furniture was arriving in about 4 weeks. They wanted to have a home ready for it. Also, they didn't want the inconvenience and extra expense of renting a motel room.

The problem was that at the time, the earliest a lender could arrange financing was 6 weeks, probably closer to 8. That meant that the buyer wanted to be in the premises for 2 to 4 weeks before the deal could close.

What's the problem here?

To see the problem I faced, you have to look at the downside risk. What if the buyer eventually couldn't get financing and the deal couldn't close? What if the buyer decided to back out of the purchase? In short, there are many scenarios that would lead to the deal not closing. Yet, if I gave possession prior to close, I'd now have people in the premises and getting them out could be a big problem.

Obviously, timing was a big deal point here and a great inconvenience for me. Why should I bother with all the hassle involved? Why not simply dump the deal?

The buyers understood the problem. So they offered me very close to full price and no other conditions—cash to new loan. I would get nearly my full price and all cash out, something I wanted and something which was a strong inducement for me to find a way to make it work.

Ultimately, I had the buyers sign a 6-month lease agreement putting up both first and last month's rent plus a substantial security/cleaning deposit outside of escrow (paid directly to me). The sales agreement stipulated, however, that if they bought the property within 8 weeks (which should be enough time for them to secure financing), all the lease money, including the deposit, became part of the down payment. If they didn't buy, then, of course they were tenants.

They were satisfied with the deal. They had a house to move into when they needed it. I was likewise satisfied. I had a pretty sure shot at a sale. And if the sale didn't go through, then I had the property rented. Since the house was a rental anyway, this fit in well with my plans.

Ultimately, the buyers did qualify, did get the mortgage, and the deal closed—a successful negotiation of time.

Trap

One of the dangers of letting a buyer in before closing is that if the deal doesn't close, the buyer then may be considered a tenant with tenant's rights. This means that if the buyer refuses to move or pay rent, you might have to go through expensive and potentially lengthy (if the buyer contests) eviction procedures to remove the buyer from the house.

Of course, this can work both ways. Sometimes a seller wants to stay after the transaction closes. Buyers have to be wary of this, lest they later have difficulty getting the former seller to leave the premises.

And there's also the problem of what condition the property will be in when a seller or buyer finally leaves even if the transaction closes. There's no opportunity here for the other party to realistically inspect prior to close, if someone is already in the house.

Wasting Time

A different concern with regard to time is that the property is usually taken off the market once buyers sign a sales agreement. If the house is off the market a month or so while the buyer hunts for a mortgage, and if ultimately the deal falls through, that's a lot of time wasted during which another potential buyer could be found. Some sellers will, therefore, negotiate a clause in the sales agreement that allows them to continue showing the property and to take backup offers until the deal closes.

For buyers, the problem here is that if they have trouble securing financing or the closing is delayed for any reason, the seller could receive another, better backup offer and they could lose the deal. Before granting permission for the seller to keep showing the property and to take backup offers, therefore, buyers should seek to negotiate a concession elsewhere.

What to Do When There Are Frivolous Contingencies

I used to know a builder who had this rule, "I don't care what the sales agreement says, as long as there's a 'subject to' in it."

He was, of course, referring to a contingency clause, a condition which made the sale subject to some action (or lack of action) occurring. While I think he was a bit careless in not caring what the clause was about, his point was well taken. Almost any contingency will weaken a sales agreement and will threaten it if there's a lawsuit and the matter gets to court.

Some buyers, well aware of this, will insist on one or more contingency clauses. This, they feel, gives them a way to back out of the deal and not have a concern over the deposit being tied up. I refer to these as frivolous contingencies.

On the other hand, sometimes the buyer is sincere, but new to real estate or simply wants to have a lot of clauses inserted because it makes him or her feel more secure. Knowing they can back out at any time may be what allows the buyers, psychologically, to make the offer.

On the other hand, from the seller's perspective, each new contingency weakens the deal. If I'm a seller and the buyers insist on, for example, making the sale subject to one spouse getting a raise from an employer or the other getting a new job in the area, I have to ask myself whether I really want to sign the deal. After all, the buyers can control the contingency. They can forget to ask for a raise or look for a new job. In short, they can back out of the deal any time they want and I'm left holding nothing.

What to Do about Contingencies

There are three ways to handle a contingency from the seller's point of view. First, verbally define it as it is—a condition which virtually makes the agreement nonbinding on the buyers only. Second, once everyone understands what a disadvantage this puts you under, negotiate for concessions. The concessions could be in the form of price and/or terms.

Finally, if you want to move forward with a sales agreement with frivolous contingencies, you should insist on the right to keep showing the property and keep accepting backup offers.

Linking Sales

A common contingency is when buyers insist on having the right first to sell their old home before they buy yours. They may want a clause inserted which says that the purchase of your home is "contingent upon the sale of their existing home."

In a hot market, few sellers would be tempted to sign such an offer. In a slow market, many sellers would. However, if you're a seller and you do, it would be wise to include a sentence or two that allowed you to keep showing the property and to take backup offers. Further, if you got a backup offer, the buyers would have, for example, 48 hours to remove the contingency or would have to back out of the deal.

In other words, yes, you'd hold your house for the buyers while they tried to sell their old home. But if you got a more solid offer, they'd have to agree to buy yours even without the sale of the old home. It's a way to have your cake and eat it too.

Finally, smart negotiators will put a time limitation on every contingency. It might be a month or a week or 72 hours, but the buyer or seller would have only a certain amount of time to act on the contingency or else it would have to be removed. For example, the buyer may want a contingency relating to a home inspection. This is perfectly natural and to be expected. However, the seller may go along only if the buyer agrees to remove the contingency *within 10 days*. This means the buyer must get the inspection report and approve of it within 10 days and sign a release of the contingency. If the buyer fails to do so, the sale is off and the seller can resell.

A purely frivolous contingency may be that the buyers want to make the deal subject to the approval of an aunt in Maryland. Maybe they rely heavily on this person's judgment.

If everything else in the deal were to my liking and the prospect of another buyer coming along soon was slim, I would agree. But I would add a time contingency. Yes, you can secure the approval of your aunt, but she has to give it within 3 days. In other words, the buyers have to remove the contingency within 72 hours to keep the deal alive.

But, they may argue, it will take longer than that for the aunt to get out here to see the house.

Fine, make it 4 days.

The point is that almost any kind of frivolous contingency can be nullified by stipulating a strict time limit. It has to be cleared within certain time parameters for the deal to continue. If it isn't cleared, there is no deal.

Tip

Remember, any time you offer a contingency, particularly a frivolous one, you are making a weaker offer and will undoubtedly have to pay for it either by having the offer rejected outright or by making concessions in price or other terms. A savvy buyer will put in as *few* contingencies as possible to get better terms and price.

Nonfrivolous Contingency

One of the most common nonfrivolous contingencies specifies that there is no deal if the buyer can't qualify for financing. It goes without saying that this should be in every sales agreement to protect the buyer.

However, I've seen some gutsy buyers in a hot market pull that contingency out! They knew they were competing with other buyers for the same property and they made a totally "noncontingent" offer. They would buy the property, period. I've even seen such buyers make the deposit check out directly to the seller!

As I said, it takes guts. As a buyer you have to be perfectly sure of your financing (or have cash) and be quite convinced you want that property no matter what. I don't suggest such an offer, however, for the faint of heart.

How Should You Handle the Final Walk-Through?

Most sales agreements today provide for a final walk-through by the buyer, usually the day before the deal closes. (When title transfers, the seller gets the money, and the buyer usually gets the house.) The reason this walk-through came about, as have so many other trends in real estate, is largely to protect agents.

In the past, buyers would not see the property, at least the inside, between the time they first made the offer and the time they finally got clear title. However, during that period the seller might have had wild parties every night. The walls might be stained with food, the floors awash in wine, the toilet fixtures ripped out. No, again, it's not likely, but believe it or not, I have seen this sort of thing happen!

When the buyers take possession, bright-eyed and anticipating a lovely new home, they are aghast at what they find. And who do they blame? The seller, of course. But also the seller's agent, who they say "should have seen that this didn't happen—should have informed us." In the past, agents have had to pay to make up for the actions of irresponsible sellers.

Therefore, to prevent the possibility of any of this happening, the "final walk-through" came into popularity. Here, the buyer is allowed to see the property just before the deal closes to be sure that it's just as it was when the offer was made.

The walk-through also has the effect of putting the sellers on notice that they had better keep the home shipshape, because it will have to pass inspection before the deal can close. The actual result of all this, however, is that agents no longer have to deal with angry buyers and partying sellers. They are largely off the hook. (If the buyers see the property just before close and accept, there is far less for them to complain about.)

The purpose of the final walk-through, therefore, is to make sure the physical condition of the property hasn't changed, and that's what's usually specified in the relevant contract clause. However, sometimes buyers see it as a last-minute opportunity to back out of the deal.

Some friends of mine were buying a townhouse near Los Angeles. (A townhouse normally is connected with another home only by common walls—there is land beneath and sky above. A condominium is more like an apartment—there are other condos above, below, and to the sides.) It was a nice property and my friends qualified for the financing. All the contingencies, except the walk-through, were removed. However, just before the sale was to close, they discovered another townhouse nearby that was bigger, cost less, and was in a better neighborhood. Naturally, they wanted out of the deal they had made so they could buy the other townhouse. However, their reasons for wanting out were not likely to appeal to the seller of the first property.

So they confronted their agent and explained their dilemma. The agent said she would "fix it." Very few agents would do this.

The agent led my friends through their final walk-through and suggested that perhaps things weren't as they had originally been. They agreed. The house was much smaller than they had originally seen it to be. Also, the painting on the walls was marked up, the carpet was worn, and the roof needed to be replaced; there were a hundred things different from when they first walked through.

The agent presented the seller with a huge list of problems with the property—problems which would have cost a fortune to fix. The seller, naturally, said that the buyers were obviously trying to back out. The property hadn't deteriorated that much since the offer was made. The agent simply said, "Maybe." Then she emphasized that the buyers were exercising their right under the final walk-through contingency. Ultimately, they just did not find the property suitable.

In this true story, the seller finally said okay and released the buyers, signing off and returning the deposit. The agent then sold my friends the other townhouse and completed the deal.

What Could the Sellers Have Done?

The seller could have insisted that the buyers complete the sale. The seller could have demanded the deposit. The trouble was the matter of that final walk-through contingency. The way it had been written, it gave the buyers the power to reject the property right up until the last minute.

The moral of this story is that if you're the seller, be very careful of a final walk-through contingency. In the vast majority of cases, they do serve the purpose of having the seller maintain the property in good condition. But in some cases they can be abused.

Trap

___

If you're a seller, have an attorney check the final walk-through contingency clause. Have the wording strengthened so that there is less chance the buyers can use it as a way to back out of the deal. Also, if you agree to such a contingency, you may want to use it as a deal point to bargain for concessions elsewhere.

___

Tip

___

If you're a buyer, remember that any contingent clause in a sales agreement weakens it. If there's a provision that says the sale is "subject to" your approval on a final walk-through, you may have the right to back out of the deal right up to the very last moment! (Check with a good lawyer first, however.) That might be worth conceding some deal points elsewhere in the transaction.

8
Offer and Counteroffer

It's important to always deal with the right person, the one who has the power to negotiate. If you're a buyer, that means going right to the seller—and vice versa.

However, while it may be a good idea and those in investment real estate will pursue it, I suspect that a great many readers who are home buyers and sellers will shy away. If you're not experienced in real estate transactions, the thought of dealing face to face can be intimidating.

There's nothing wrong with feeling this way. Indeed, it's important that you know how you feel so you don't get in over your head. If you're more comfortable dealing at arm's length through an agent, fine. In this chapter we'll see how to negotiate through offer and counteroffer, using the agent as the intermediary.

What Do You Say to Your Agent?

When you buy a house and deal exclusively with an agent, you probably won't see the seller except, perhaps, when you tour the home. The only person you'll see will be the agent. This approach has pluses and drawbacks. On the plus side, you can vent your feelings about the house and the seller and not worry about offending the other party. You can openly complain that the seller is a miserable housekeeper and you wouldn't keep a dog in a place in that condition. The agent will never mention it to the seller.

On the other hand, all the information that you get about the other party comes from the agent. If your broker isn't perceptive or leaves things out, you could get a skewed perspective about the seller that, for example, leads you to accept an offer for too little or to counter for too much.

Who Is Your Agent Working For?

Be sure you keep in mind who your agent is working for. Technically, a seller's agent can't reveal to the buyer information that would weaken the seller. For example, a seller's agent can't reveal that the seller has said, "I'd be willing to sell for $10,000 less than I'm asking," unless the seller authorizes the agent to say this. Similarly, a buyer's agent can't reveal to the seller the buyer's top price for the property, unless authorized.

Further, if you're a buyer working with a seller's agent, beware of telling the agent that although you're making an offer for one price, you'd actually be willing to pay $10,000 more. The agent is ethically bound to reveal that information to the seller! The same holds true in reverse for a buyer's agent.

Therefore, as a buyer, you frequently need to use your best negotiating tactics both on the seller and on the agent. This means that you will want to hold your cards fairly close to your vest.

Yes, ask the agent for opinions both on the true value of the property and on the amount to offer. Yes, consider carefully what the agent says and then ask the agent what he or she would do in your situation.

But always take a moment to come away and weigh what has been said against the agent's scale of competence, the fiduciary responsibilities of the agent (briefly described in the Trap above), and common sense. Ultimately, you need to make your own decision.

Tip

The only person you can count on to be 100 percent on your side in a real estate transaction is you. (See Rule 3.)

What's the Procedure for Offers?

When you're dealing through an agent, offers and counteroffers are presented in written form. (When you're dealing face to face, often only the original offer is written—then you sit down with the other party and negotiate in person from there.) You make an offer and the agent, in consultation, writes it out on a sales agreement. Then the agent presents the offer to the other party and, presumably, argues your case for you.

If the offer is accepted, fine. You've got a deal. However, I suspect that in better than 80 percent of real estate transactions, the buyer's original offer is not accepted. Instead, the seller counteroffers. The agent will then come back and explain the seller's position, may even argue for accepting the seller's counteroffer, or may make suggestions about countering the counter.

Tip

Remember the concept of a package—the counter may, for example, maintain the seller's original price, but offer better terms or time. (It is possible for the seller to counter at exactly the originally asked price and terms—a "take it or leave it" counter.)

Offer and Counteroffer

1. The buyer makes an offer which the agent writes up. The offer usually has a time limit for acceptance.
2. As soon as possible, the agent presents the offer to the seller.

3. The seller accepts the offer exactly as written up, or rejects it.

4. If the seller rejects the offer, he or she may choose to counter. The counter will presumably be for less than the seller originally wanted, but more than the buyer offered. The counter will also usually have a time limit for acceptance.

5. The buyer may now accept or reject the seller's offer. The buyer, however, is under no obligation to accept any counteroffer from the seller.

6. The buyer may choose to counter the counteroffer.

7. The offer-and-counteroffer process can continue almost indefinitely. There are no limits to the number of times the negotiations can go back and forth.

Tip

Remember, the agent is now negotiating for you. If the agent is skilled and determined, you have a much better chance of getting any offer accepted. That's why it's important at the onset to pick agents who you believe are good negotiators, not just friendly faces. (See Rule 2 in Chap. 1 about not having a "nice" agent.)

If you're going to counter, it's usually a good idea to make the counter on the same document as the original offer. The reason is psychological. Even though the other party knows that the original offer was rejected, placing the counter on the same document makes it seem like the same deal is still being negotiated. The procedure holds through for counter counters. Better to wear out the paper on a sales agreement than lose the deal.

Why Would a Buyer Want a Counteroffer?

In Chap. 5 we discussed how much to offer for a property and the importance of making a serious offer that the seller can accept. In a great many instances in which a deal is actually made, the seller's counter contains only minor changes.

However, sometimes a buyer may not really expect the seller to accept an original offer. Indeed, the buyer may make a "lowball" offer so far below the asking price or with such inferior terms that the buyer knows no reasonable seller will accept it. Why would a buyer make such an offer to a seller? The reason is that the buyer may want the seller to counteroffer.

There are many reasons for wanting a counteroffer, including:

1. The seller has an unrealistically high asking price. By making an unrealistically low offer, you, the buyer, hope to compromise somewhere in between.

2. You simply can't afford anywhere near what the seller is asking. So you offer something close to your maximum, hoping the seller will be desperate enough to counter near your offer.

3. You simply want to "steal" the property. When the seller counters, you'll again offer close to your initial low price, hoping that by now the seller will be discouraged enough to accept.

4. You simply want to get the negotiations opened. Once offers are flying through the air, you hope to learn enough about the seller to determine the best price you can get.

Why Would a Seller Want to Counter?

As a seller represented by an agent, you don't really have a handle on what kind of person the buyer is. (That's the reason I recommend face to face negotiations.) Rather, you have to judge in part by what the agent reports, but mainly by what the buyer does. You have to watch the buyer's actions, and these come in the form of an offer.

Not long ago a friend of mine was selling a house which was in dire straits. The house was on a steep hillside built on an old streambed. During the rainy season that stream came back to life, and over the years it had eroded much of the foundation of my friend's home. The house now teetered precariously on what was left of the foundation. My friend knew that her only chance of selling was to find a buyer who would be willing to take the property "as is" and fix it.

Any time you see a house advertised "as is," you can figure it has big problems. Although some agents advise all sellers to sell "as is" as a way of protecting themselves against buyers later coming back with a lawsuit claiming that some defect wasn't disclosed, I don't believe such a course of action will work. Whether a house is sold "as is" or not, the seller still has to disclose all defects to the buyer. All that happens when a seller tries to sell "as is" is that the buyer is put on notice that there's something seriously wrong with the property. As a result, the buyer will probably want to offer much less for it.

Tip

If you're a seller, it's much better, in my opinion, not to sell "as is." Just disclose all problems, and if there's something in particular that you don't want to warrant (guarantee), make sure the buyers sign off as being aware of that particular defect when they accept the property.

Not surprisingly, my friend with the hillside house got several purchase offers for a ridiculously low price. She countered, including a paragraph in the sales agreement which said the buyer was fully aware of the foundation problems and accepted them. She also asked a higher price.

The first two buyers who offered were scared away by the counter. They had hoped (without much reason) that the seller either would sell just for the value of the land or would fix the problem as part of the sale.

The third buyer, however, had experience in building construction and was fascinated by the challenge posed by my friend's house. He accepted the paragraph regarding the foundation problems and proceeded to negotiate a price that he felt would be justified given the condition of the property. My friend, the seller, had achieved her objective of finding a buyer who could handle the problem and would not want so low a price as to be buying the land only. Ultimately, after going back and forth five times, a deal was signed.

The Three Types of Offers

Buyers can make three kinds of offers:

Lowball.   The offer is ridiculously below what the seller is asking. The usual hope is that the seller will counter at a compromise price.

"Close to asking."   The buyer simply wants the property and is willing to pay the seller's price. However, the buyer is hoping that the seller will come down a little rather than chance simply rejecting or countering the buyer's offer.

Compromise.   The buyer comes in somewhere in between, looking for a series of counters.

The Two Types of Counters

Sellers really have only two realistic choices in making a counteroffer:

Highball.   The seller rejects the buyer's offer and comes back almost to the asking price. The seller's motivation here is simply to keep the negotiations open in the hope that the buyer will eventually "come around."

Compromise.   The seller counters somewhere in between the asking price and the buyer's offer. The seller is hoping that negotiations via a series of counters will eventually result in an acceptable price.

To my mind, there's little point in the seller countering a buyer's "close to asking" offer. It's better to simply accept it than run the risk of the buyer simply walking away in a huff. On the other hand, some hard-nosed sellers will simply counter such an offer by writing in the exact asking price and terms.

Sometimes they win and get a deal. But sometimes the buyer gets offended and walks.

Trap

Beware of an agent who comes back after presenting your offer (or counteroffer) and says, "We have a deal. Congratulations! Oh, by the way. The other party made a few minor changes and I'll come by and have you initial them."

That's incorrect. Any changes at all mean the offer (or counter) was rejected. You now no longer have any obligations to the deal. When the agent comes by for "initialing" what's really being presented to you is a totally new counteroffer.

The Bottom Line

My best advice in offering and counteroffering is to strive continuously to keep the negotiations open. I've countered what I thought were hopeless offers, only to have the other party rethink its position and come back with something more realistic.

9
Leveraging the Inspection Report

Recently I received a letter from a couple who had purchased an earlier *Tips and Traps* book in which I mentioned that when buying a home, it is possible to use an inspection report to get a better price. They reported that they had done so and had gotten a price reduction of $16,500 on a $112,000 offer.

They explained that they had made the offer on a home in a mountainous area. They had gotten the best deal they could and had included a contingency that the transaction was subject to their approving a home inspection.

The couple hired a retired engineer to give the inspection and he had concluded that the house had a bad foundation. Parts of it were cracked and some serious repair work needed to be done. In addition, because of the weakened foundation, several perimeter wall areas were sagging and needed to be fixed.

Armed with the report, the buyers had leveraged the seller into reducing his price by nearly 15 percent. They had purchased the property and they had been able to get the repair work done for a fraction of the estimated cost. Needless to say, they were thrilled with the deal.

How Leveraging the
Inspection Report Works

It's important to understand that today nearly all real estate transfers in most parts of the country include a home inspection. As noted earlier, the first and most obvious reason is that buyers want a better handle on what they are purchasing. Most purchasers simply do not have the knowledge to determine the condition of a property. Therefore, they are willing to pay an inspector to take a look and give them a report.

The inspection report is often made *after* the deal is signed. This means that when negotiations take place, the true condition of the property is typically unknown.

Therefore, savvy buyers make the deal *contingent* upon their approving the inspection report. If the report comes out bad, they can back out of the deal with no harm to themselves. As noted in Chap. 4, sellers can protect themselves by putting a time limit on the buyer's approval. The buyer has 7 to 10 days (or however long) to approve the report, or else the deal is gone and the seller can accept other offers. (Remember Rule 19 about setting a deadline.)

Preinspected Homes

Sometimes sellers will have an inspection prior to finding a buyer. They may even advertise, "Home Is Preinspected."

Often this happens when there is a deal that falls through and a would-be buyer paid to have an inspection. The seller now has a copy of that report and makes it available to the next would-be buyer. (Normally, the seller must make all such reports available.) The seller usually hopes the buyer will accept this report and sign off on a deal without contingencies.

The problem here is that if you're the buyer, you really don't know under what circumstances the previous report was made. Did the inspector do a competent job? Did the previous would-be buyer go along and ask questions and point out potential problems? (Often the verbal explanations of a home inspector are the most revealing and helpful part of the process.)

Therefore, I always suggest you have your own inspection (and pay for it—usually under $300) along with a contingency pertaining to it. Yes, accept a previous report and read it—with a grain of salt. But until your own inspector is out there, you along with him, you really don't have a true handle on the property's condition.

Do Sellers Want a Home Inspection?

A not so obvious reason for a home inspection is that sellers likewise want it. This is largely because of our litigious society, which has seen an alarming rise in the number of buyers who have successfully sued sellers for either damages or rescission (cancellation of the deal, with the seller returning the buyer's money and taking back the property) because of undisclosed defects. With a formal inspection, however, the seller can point out that every effort was made to reveal the true condition of the property; therefore, the purchaser has less recourse if a problem is later discovered. (Agents likewise love a formal inspection, because otherwise they are frequently the ones blamed when the buyer discovers a defect.)

Value as Condition

As a result, the inspection report becomes a valuable discovery tool for both buyer and seller. It also can be a vital negotiating tool. Remember, first, that the value of a home is determined to a large extent by the condition of the physical structure itself. (The lot and location are the other parts of the value.) Therefore, when you buy a home, the price you're paying includes, presumably, a house in good shape—except for any problems disclosed by the seller.

In fact, when you as a buyer make an offer and negotiate a sale, you assume that the house is okay except for whatever defects the seller discloses. Defects—which can be problems as severe as foundation cracks or as minor as chipping paint—

change what you are buying and, hence, affect the price you are (or should be) willing to pay.

Tip

In most states today, the seller gives the buyer a disclosure statement (describing all defects in the property) at or near the time the sales agreement is signed. The buyer is then given a chance to pull back on the deal. In California, for example, the buyer has 3 days after receiving the disclosure in which to back out of the deal with no penalty. The sooner the buyer receives the disclosure, the sooner the backing-out period ends.

How to Leverage During Negotiations

There are two times that an inspection report can leverage a better deal. The first is when the deal is originally negotiated. Usually this happens when the seller already has previously had the house inspected.

If the seller has an existing inspection report, it may reveal defects or problems. As a buyer, you may point these out and use them as arguments to leverage a lower price. On the other hand, the seller may have already taken these defects into account, as reflected in a lower asking price. As a buyer, you may counter that more off is justified.

On the other hand, a seller can also use an inspection report as leverage. For example, the seller may point out that since an existing inspection report revealed few or no problems, the buyer shouldn't hesitate to offer more for the property. In a sense, the buyer already has assurances of the soundness of the home. (Savvy buyers, as noted above, will still insist on their own report, with a contingency referring to it in the sales agreement.)

Tip

A seller with an existing inspection report has some justification in resisting a new inspection from the buyer, saying it will just slow down the deal. Further, if the buyer insists on an inspection contingency, the seller with an existing report may counter that it's a deal point and ask for concessions elsewhere.

The other time that an inspection can be used to leverage a better deal is after the report has been made. It's at this point that negotiations may actually be reopened.

Sally and Ted were buying a home that the seller represented to them as being in "perfect condition." It certainly looked sharp, with beautiful landscaping in front, a new paint job, and a pleasing rustic backyard. But just to be safe, they insisted on an inspection and made the deal contingent upon their approving it. The seller said, "Sure." After all, he felt the property was terrific.

Sally and Ted hired a former building inspector to conduct the examination for them. He had been around construction all his life, and because of his inspection experience he claimed to know just what to look for.

The inspection took about 4 hours—probably twice as long as most—and revealed a whole laundry list of problems: some minor, some more severe. For example, the gas forced-air furnace had a hole in the heat exchanger. It would probably have to be replaced. The plumbing under the sink in one bathroom was nearly rotted out and also would have to be replaced. Worse, the chimney had cracked and would need to be rebuilt. Worst of all, the wood-shingled roof, which appeared fine from the ground, actually had a number of shingles missing. Looking up from underneath in the attic, the inspector uncovered many cracks and holes. He recommended having the roof replaced.

The seller was aghast at the report and, quite frankly, so were Sally and Ted. They had thought they were buying a home in great condition. Now it turned out that the house had severe problems. Sally and Ted said they wanted to get a handle on how much cost was involved, so they hired several contractors to come in quickly and give them bids on repair and replacement work. The total was in excess of $24,000.

Now they went back to the negotiating table. They said they wanted the work done and the seller to pay for it. The seller stubbornly refused. He said it was too much money. He simply wouldn't do it. Let them back out of the deal. He'd sell it to someone else.

Sally pointed out that in any future deals the seller would have to reveal the inspection report, and any other buyer would just as likely want the work done. Further, Ted casually mentioned that if the seller hid the report, he was opening himself up for a tremendous lawsuit from a new buyer. The seller decided to rethink his position. Eventually, the seller had the chimney, furnace, and plumbing fixed (for substantially less than Sally and Ted's original estimates). And he gave them $10,000 off the price for the bad roof.

Once the deal went through, and Sally and Ted moved in, Ted got several flats of shingles, went out on the roof, and over a weekend made repairs himself. The total cost was under $500. Of course, it was not a new roof and would eventually need to be replaced. But it would be usable for several more years without leaking. Two years later they resold the property, revealing that the existing roof was old and weathered but did not leak. An inspection subsequently showed that no shingles were missing and no light shone through cracks visible from below (thanks to Ted's efforts). The next buyer bought the property without quibbling over the roof.

The important point here is that the inspection report allowed the negotiations to reopen at a later date. By then the seller had a great deal of time invested in the deal and was psychologically committed to going through with it. The report allowed the buyers to convince the seller to lower the price. The inspection report thus became a vital tool for the buyer in leveraging price.

Dealing with Lenders

There are important financing considerations that need to be taken into account whenever the price is lowered after the sales agreement has been signed. Basically, they revolve around the fact that lenders do not want to make loans on properties that need repair work. In order to get the financing, the work normally has to be completed first. For example, the inspection report may say that the chimney has to be rebuilt. If buyer and seller now sign an addendum to the sales agreement saying that the seller will have the chimney rebuilt, the lender will normally want proof of the work having been done before the loan can be funded. This will be a contingency the lender will add to the loan.

On the other hand, if the addendum says that the seller will pay $8000 back to the buyer (or give the buyer credit for that amount) to compensate for the work that needs to be done on the chimney, the lender may not fund at all, again insisting that the work be done before the deal is concluded and escrow closes.

In other words, any time the sales agreement reflects a repair to the property, the lender usually insists the repair be done before the deal is concluded. This could preclude a reduction in sales price as compensation for a broken or damaged part of the house.

Tip

Many times the cost of the repair work is variable. Two contractors may have widely differing bids. And if the owners do the work themselves, the cost may be only that of building materials. This is one good reason the seller may want to seriously consider doing work in lieu of reducing price.

Whether work reported on an inspection report needs to be done or not is often a matter of opinion. The buyer may say, yes, the seller, no. In such cases (as with the roof noted above), it is sometimes preferable to reduce the sales price of the property without reference to the specific reason. In other words, having looked at the inspection report, buyer and seller have renegotiated and determined that the original price was too high. As a consequence, they have set it lower. The sale no longer is contingent upon the roof being repaired. In some cases, this will satisfy a lender.

Buyers Who "Set Up" Sellers

Buyers can and do set up sellers, although the practice is not principled. Also, if the sellers find out, the deal can be lost or the negotiations can become much more difficult. As a seller, you should try to be aware of these "setups."

Joan found a home she wanted to buy. It was owned free and clear by two elderly people who were planning to move into a much smaller condo. Joan gave the house a thorough inspection on her own. Since she had a degree in architecture, she had an excellent feel for what might be wrong with a property, and detected a serious problem. During Joan's inspection, she noted that the house followed the steep slope of the hill on one side. In other words, the house was actually lower on the west side, where the hill fell away, than on the right. As a result, there were some subtle stress cracks in the foundation and quite a few small cracks on the walls inside. The elderly sellers, who had lived there for years, had never noticed the gradual changes in the property; they felt the relatively minor cracks in the interior walls were due to "natural settling." Their real estate agent didn't realize there was a problem either.

Joan never brought her concerns into the open. Instead, she negotiated the best price as if the house had no defects. She did, however, insist on a home inspection and made the deal contingent upon her approving the report. The sellers, feeling all was well, congratulated themselves on a sale and turned around and bought a condo they had been eyeing.

Joan hired a structural engineer to inspect the property. He quickly discovered the defect and noted it in the inspection report. Then Joan called out the most expensive construction company in the area to give a bid on repairs. Finally, armed with the report and the bid, she called on the sellers.

Joan's bid for repairs was fully a third of the sales price! The sellers were shocked. But the inspection report had been conducted by a highly reputable inspector, as their own agent noted. And the construction company which gave the bid was one of the best in the area. So the sellers felt they could not reasonably challenge the report or the costs of repair.

Further, by now the sellers had committed to purchasing another home. If they were to back out of Joan's deal, they would lose out on the smaller retirement condo they wanted. Finally, they felt that no matter who the buyer was, they would have to reduce the price substantially. (The alternative of having the work done themselves was simply too overwhelming for them.) In the end, they agreed to a one-third price reduction.

Joan quickly bought the property and moved in. She's still living there and hasn't done any repair work. After all, there was nothing dangerous about the condition. She has patted herself on the back many times about her shrewd investment. On the other hand, the sellers were out a considerable amount of money which they had counted on using for their retirement.

The "Aboveboard" Approach

Had Joan played her cards aboveboard, she might have noted the problem with the house at the time she made her offer. Indeed, she might have made a lower offer initially because of it.

As a result, the sellers would have been made aware and might have hired their own inspector to check it out. Further, they might have gotten bids from several contractors—bids that could have been significantly lower than the bid Joan got. And because the sellers could have acted during the initial negotiations, they wouldn't have been committed to buying another house and would have felt free to turn Joan down if her offer was too low. In short, if Joan had been strictly straightforward, she probably would never have been able to leverage the price as low as she did on the basis of her inspection report.

Some may conclude that Joan was simply a shrewd buyer. However, I do not personally approve of her approach and do not advocate or condone it. Further, I strongly believe that "what goes around, comes around." In my own life, I've witnessed a certain symmetry, justice, balance—or whatever you might want to call it—to the universe. If you cheat someone, that will come back to haunt you.

In Joan's case (obviously not her real name), the pendulum did swing back. I saw her nearly 10 years later when she was trying to resell the property. By then, the erosion on the side of the house with the steep slope had accelerated and much of the foundation had severely cracked. There was no mistaking, to anyone who looked, that a severe problem existed here. Indeed, seeking to protect himself from any liability, the real estate agent called in a city inspector, who promptly condemned the house!

The upshot was that while the lot remained valuable, the house had to be completely torn down. In the end, Joan got less for the property, after 10 years, than she originally paid for it.

Trap

In this true example, Joan really did take advantage of elderly sellers, although probably not in a way that could get her into serious trouble. However, in general, especially when dealing with elderly people in real estate, it is important not to exert "undue influence." That simply means not to take advantage of other people through your relationship with them.

If you get a better deal because of a defect with the house, get the defect fixed. Recall that in our earlier example, Ted and Sally got $10,000 off the price because of a problem roof. However, Ted did repair the roof (though not replace it) and was able to do so for far less money. If Joan had taken care of the settling problem when she purchased the house, she probably would not have had a major problem years later.

The Bottom Line

The home inspection report can be a useful negotiating tool to leverage price in a real estate deal. However, it can also be double-edged. Sometimes it can help the buyer—and other times, the seller.

10
How to Negotiate with a Lender

Most people believe that you can't negotiate with lenders. You take what they have to offer or not. It's that simple. For example, Carmen was buying her first home, a condo, and needed to secure financing. The price was $140,000 and she wanted to put no more than 10 percent down. That meant that she needed a 90 percent loan.

She went to a mortgage broker, who told her that while he could indeed secure a 90 percent mortgage, it would cost her half of one percent above the current market rate. According to the broker, she had a blemish on her credit and couldn't get a "conforming" loan; thus, he'd have to go to a "portfolio" lender. (A *conforming loan* meets or conforms to mortgage underwriter standards for sale to the secondary market—usually to a government mortgage institution like Fannie Mae or Freddie Mac— it is the least expensive type of loan. A *portfolio loan* is made directly by a lender who usually intends to hold it and not sell it on the secondary market—usually a more expensive loan.)

Further, the broker wanted 3 points (3 percent of the mortgage) as a loan fee plus another $900 in origination costs. And he wanted $1035 up front for handling the financing. (The $1000 was an advance on the loan fees, the $35 was for a credit report.)

Not knowing any better, Carmen agreed. The mortgage broker seemed to take forever to get the loan, but he finally did. Only when it came time to sign did Carmen discover that the loan was an extra one-quarter of one percent higher (and an extra half point higher) than the broker originally claimed.

She protested, but the broker pointed out that the market had changed and this was the best he could do. Joan said she wasn't satisfied and would go elsewhere. He smiled and replied that she was free to do that. But he had secured financing for her and was entitled to the $1035 he had originally charged, whether she took the loan or not. Further, to go somewhere else meant having to start the whole financing process over again. He wondered aloud if the seller would be willing to wait several more weeks for her to secure a mortgage somewhere else.

In the end Carmen took the loan, paid the extra costs, and got the condo she wanted.

Tip

As noted earlier, the Real Estate Settlement Procedures Act (RESPA) requires lenders to give borrowers a preliminary statement of their costs for a mortgage. Read this statement carefully, as it should reveal most of the "garbage" fees the lender may be charging.

When to Negotiate for a Mortgage

Carmen's problems (again a true story, by the way) stem from several misconceptions on her part. Like most people, she believed there was no possibility of negotiating with the lender. Then, when she was delivered an unattractive mortgage that she didn't want, she attempted to negotiate anyway, to get the mortgage broker to change the terms. By that time it was too late.

The truth is that everything in real estate is up for negotiation, including financing. The idea is to do the negotiations up front, not at the back end. At the beginning, when you first approach a mortgage broker (or direct lender such as a bank), you have the leverage. You can easily walk out and try somewhere else. You hold the high cards.

However, once the mortgage is ready to fund, you are at a disadvantage because you need the loan to close the deal and usually don't have time to begin searching elsewhere. Now the lender holds the high cards.

Lock-Ins

Negotiate all the terms of the mortgage when you first approach the mortgage broker or lender. Then get a lock-in that hopefully guarantees what you agreed upon. Sometimes in a volatile market, however, lenders won't honor their own lock-ins. To help reduce problems, get the lock-in in writing and still keep your fingers crossed.

Remember, there is no such thing as a guaranteed lock-in. For example, interest rates may rise dramatically between the time you apply for the mortgage and the time to actually fund it. Perhaps they started at 7 percent and now they're at 8 percent. Your lender gave you a written 45-day lock-in at 7 percent. That means that you have 45 days to close in order to get that rate.

You're ready to close in 40 days and demand the mortgage. The lender smiles and say okay. But there are delays. Your documents get lost in the mail. Suddenly a problem over your credit arises. Before you know it, it's 46 days. Astonishingly, the documents previously lost suddenly reappear and the credit blemish vanishes. But the lender sadly says that it's past your lock-in time, so now the rate is higher.

The truth is no one, including a lender, wants to lose money. And if a little shuffling of paper or maybe a smudge on a credit report can keep that from happening, many will seize the opportunity. A reputable lender, of course, will honor a mortgage lock-in no matter what. The trouble is, you usually don't know how reputable your lender is until it's too late.

How to Negotiate a Mortgage

To put yourself in a position to negotiate with a lender, you have to remember that the lender is not doing you any kind of favor by loaning you money. It is (or should be) a mutually beneficial transaction. You need money, the lender needs interest. If your needs match, it's a deal. Strictly business.

Thus, when you march into a mortgage broker or a direct lender's office, you're on equal footing. You need each other.

Tip

It's usually more difficult to negotiate with a direct lender such as a bank or savings and loan, because most times you don't get the opportunity to talk to the right person. You usually talk to a loan salesperson who simply mouths the lender's policy. "We have loan A, loan B, or loan C. Take your pick."

If you can get in to see an officer who has discretionary powers, you may be able to secure a loan tailored to your needs. That's why it's sometimes best to deal with a small lending institution instead of a giant one.

Conforming or Nonconforming?

Perhaps the first thing to negotiate is whether or not you qualify for a conforming loan. As noted earlier, a conforming loan is one which the lender will sell to an underwriter—usually a quasi-government corporation, such as Freddie Mac or Fannie Mae. As of this writing, these mortgages cannot be for more than $204,300. Further, the underwriter sets the parameters of the loan—the down payment, minimum credit, and other qualifications. The lender then resells large groups of these loans on the secondary market. Generally, the interest rate is set by the terms of that bulk sale.

Thus, if you go for a conforming loan (because it usually is the best deal out there), there's very little leeway to negotiate with the lender. But there is *some*. For one thing, you can argue over the garbage fees—the largely unnecessary costs that many lenders tack on to boost their profits. The lender must give you an estimate of these as soon as you apply for the loan.

For another, you can negotiate the mix of interest rate and points. (Remember, a point is equal to 1 percent of the mortgage amount and is paid up front.) As a rule of thumb, one point equals one-fourth of a percent in interest. Thus, if you want to lower the interest rate, you can offer to pay more points. Paying four additional points can lower your interest rate by roughly 1 percent. On the other hand, by paying a higher interest rate, you can reduce the points, often to zero.

Tip

What the lender is actually looking for is *yield*. This is the true return on the mortgage from all sources, including points and rate. It is close to what banks and credit card companies list as the APR, or annual percentage rate. Usually, the lender has to get a certain yield for conforming mortgages. As long as you can give that yield, you can often jostle the mix used to get it in a variety of ways.

While there is a minimum yield that the lender must get (or else lose money), there is no maximum yield. Thus, lenders will ask as much as the competition will bear. When there is a strong demand for mortgages, lenders often insist on a higher yield. On the other hand, when mortgage financing is slow, they will often take less. In many ways, it's just like negotiating with a seller. The amount of leverage you have is determined in large part by market conditions.

Check Out the Market

Check out the mortgage finance market just as you check out the real estate market. The real estate sections of local papers often report on the volume of financing. Also, local real estate brokers can tell about this market, as can mortgage brokers—who often are quite candid about conditions.

If you hear that new loans and refinancing are at all-time highs, figure you have little room to negotiate. On the other hand, if you read that lenders are laying off people because there is so little financing, your negotiating room just took a big jump.

Your ability to negotiate a portfolio (nonconforming) loan may be significantly better. A financial institution may keep nonconforming loans in its loan portfolio (hence the name). Or it may sell them in a package to insurance companies, savings and loan associations, or other lenders, often out of state. If your loan is to be resold, then again you're up against the underwriter's parameters. However, these are often less strict than those for the government mortgage organizations. If the lender is going to hold the mortgage itself, then the parameters are determined by the lender...and may be widely negotiable.

For example, a savings and loan may be willing, even anxious, to lend you $300,000 to purchase a $400,000 triplex (three residential units) if you agree to live in one of the units. If it's a relatively small lender, you may work your way upward until you actually get a chance to talk with several of the officers who sit on the loan committee.

You may negotiate interest rate, points, term (length of loan), and other costs with these officers. At this level, they may be surprisingly flexible. With more and more institutions holding on to nonconforming real estate loans over the past few years, many smaller lenders are eager to make secure loans, often to the point of being highly competitive. If you're a good wheeler and dealer and can show why yours is a particularly secure loan, you may even get a below-market rate!

Do They Want to Loan You Money?

The bottom line is that when you go to a lender—be it a bank, savings and loan, credit union, mortgage banker, or some other institution—it's not that you're asking for a favor. Lenders want to extend mortgages. After all, that's how they make their profit. If there are no borrowers, they are out of business.

Keep in mind that any lender wants to give you a mortgage until you come up with a reason not to. If your credit is good, the property qualifies, and your income is adequate, you're a good potential borrower. It's going to be hard for the lender to dismiss you over a few dollars' worth of garbage fees.

11
Negotiating Your Way Out of Foreclosure

Over the past few years, with the deep recession that has affected many parts of the country, many hardworking people who never before had a credit blemish in their lives were suddenly faced with losing their homes through foreclosure. By 1992 the rate of foreclosure nationwide was at the highest point since the Great Depression of the 1930s.

Fortunately, since then things have brightened considerably. As of this writing, the percentage of total mortgages that are in default by 30 days is only around 4.3 percent, actually quite low. The number of foreclosures is likewise down.

However, there are still pockets of deep recession in the country, and every day many Americans face the prospect of foreclosure. If it's happening to you now, or if it ever does, you'll quickly realize how sobering a situation it is.

The Consequences of Foreclosure

Before discussing methods of negotiating out of foreclosure, let's take a quick look at the consequences if you do nothing.

The emotional and psychological damage wreaked by losing your home can, of course, be devastating. However, here we're primarily concerned with financial damage.

The foreclosure process varies from state to state. In general, it always involves a period of time during which the borrower can make up back payments and correct any *default,* or failure to meet the obligations he or she has under the mortgage.

After that time period, there is either a *judicial foreclosure,* in which the lender goes to court to secure title to the borrower's home, or a *trust deed sale,* in which the lender uses an independent third party, a trustee, to gain title to the property without going to court. (Most states today use the trust deed method because of the speed—as little time as 60 days—and the reduced cost to the lender.)

That's the procedure. What's important to realize is that if you're late even once on your mortgage payment, most lenders will report that to a credit agency and it will appear on your credit record as a late payment. While one late payment usually won't damage your credit too badly (we'll see an exception in a moment), a series of late payments will.

If you stop making payments altogether and the lender goes through the entire foreclosure process, a report of that will also make its way to a credit agency. The importance of a foreclosure on a credit record cannot be underemphasized. Generally speaking, *no* institutional lender (bank, S&L, mortgage banker, insurance company, and so on) will offer another mortgage to anyone who has a foreclosure on his or her record.

Trap

Mortgage lenders are highly sensitive to late mortgage payments. To get the best loans today—generally speaking, these are conforming loans underwritten by Fannie Mae or Freddie Mac—you cannot have any blemishes on your credit, not even one late mortgage payment.

How long does this "rule" hold? Certainly for several years; in some cases forever! While a foreclosure will inhibit the ability to get credit from any source, it has a particularly bad effect on mortgage lenders. However, by gradually reestablishing credit through credit cards and by buying property for which a seller finances the sale or you assume an existing mortgage that doesn't require qualifying, you can restore your good credit. One major lender told me that after 10 years of perfect credit, with a letter giving a reasonable explanation for an earlier foreclosure (sickness, unemployment, and so on), it would offer a new mortgage to a person who had lost his or her home through foreclosure.

Thus, while a foreclosure may not be the end of the world, it's still not a very good thing to have happen.

Trap

Lenders are concerned mainly with defaults in their specific area. For example, if you default on a credit card, it may be difficult to get other credit card lenders to offer you a new card. Similarly, if you have a foreclosure, it will be extremely difficult to get mortgage lenders to offer you a new loan, although credit card lenders may be more lenient.

Tip

Whatever you do, if you ever plan to buy another home, don't let your house go to foreclosure. Borrow to make that payment, sell the property at a loss, but don't let them foreclose.

What Can You Do When You're in Default?

Most of us today know of someone who lost his or her house to foreclosure in the not too distant past. It has become that common. However, here's a story that's been told less often.

Jill and Mike were secure in a comfortable home in the Los Angeles area and both had good jobs. However, Mike was in aerospace and with the end of the cold war and the downsizing of the military, his company laid off tens of thousands of people, Mike included. Further, since other defense contractors were doing the same, he could not find other work to fit his job skills.

But he kept trying. Mike had some severance pay and Jill was still working as a computer programmer for a high-tech company. Thus, they managed to get by and pay all their bills, including their rather hefty mortgage payment of $1520 a month. However, about a year after Mike was laid off, Jill's company closed its door and she was without work as well. Now they were in a real financial pickle.

For a few months they hung on. But without Jill's income, they couldn't make that big mortgage payment.

On the first day of the first month that they couldn't make their home payment, Mike called the lender and asked to talk to someone in the foreclosure department. He explained to a representative of the lender what his predicament was and said he simply did not have enough money to make the loan payment.

The representative checked Mike and Jill's payment history and saw that they had never been late. He chuckled and noted that the payment wasn't due until the middle of the month. "Don't worry," he told them. "Something will turn up."

Mike was surprised at the lender's cavalier attitude, so he followed up the phone call with a letter explaining his situation. Next, he put the house up for sale. However, the real estate agent explained that there were an enormous number of listings just then, with many lenders offering foreclosed properties for sale. As it turned out, Mike's house was probably worth less than he owed. She said that meant he was "upside down." Yes, she would list it. But she felt that it might be quite awhile before a buyer appeared.

In Default

When Mike was nearly a month overdue on his payment, the lender's loan default department called to find out if he knew. Had the payment gotten lost in the mail?

Mike said he had called earlier and again explained his situation. He was told he'd be called back. Later that day another representative called to let Mike know how serious it was to let payments slip. Again Mike explained his situation and again he followed up the conversation with a letter.

A few weeks later, Mike got a letter from a credit-reporting agency notifying him that the lender had sent in a notice that he had missed a payment. The agency wanted to know if he disputed the claim. He responded that he did not, but included a letter of explanation.

Things went on in this manner for nearly 3 months. During that time neither Mike nor Jill found work. Worse, no buyers or even lookers stopped by their home.

Then one day Mike got a call from the lender. A representative, Bill, wanted to know how he was coming along in finding work or selling his house. Mike told him the sad news. Bill then asked Mike if he could send him a copy of the listing agreement showing that the house was for sale. The lender needed it immediately. Mike got a copy and sent it out.

Two days later Bill called back and said he'd like a printout from the real estate agent showing comparable sales over the past 6 months to see if Mike was pricing his house at market. Mike immediately got the agent to send it out. Actually, his house was then priced high enough just to pay the costs of sale and the mortgage. If it sold, Mike and Jill would get nothing out of it. And still there were no buyers.

A week later Bill called back and wanted proof that Mike and his wife were really out of work. Mike did have an old termination slip from his last job and asked if a copy of a recent unemployment check to his wife would suffice. Bill said they would.

A week later Bill called again and said that if Mike couldn't make up the payments, the lender would be forced to start formal foreclosure proceedings. That meant that Mike would lose his home in about 4 months. Mike and Jill asked for a meeting.

Facing Foreclosure

At the meeting with Bill and several other representatives of the lender, Mike and Jill explained the situation as they saw it. Their fields had changed and they couldn't presently find work. There was a recession on and no houses in the area were selling. Yes, the lender could foreclose, but if it did, it would end up with a house it couldn't resell. As it stood now, even if Mike and Jill sold, they wouldn't get any money out of the deal anyway. Further, they carefully pointed out that if the lender foreclosed, it would end up with a house that was worth less than the mortgage amount, a house which it in all likelihood couldn't sell either.

The lender's representatives grimaced at that. Then they offered Mike a proposition. They said they would allow him to skip the next three payments if after that he made up all the interest on all the payments he had missed. They would even offer him a plan of slightly higher payments to help make up what he owed.

Mike explained that he didn't think he could make up any payments until he found a job. But he would try. They agreed.

Three months later Mike's situation hadn't changed and he asked for another meeting with the lender. After he explained his situation, he asked if the lender could simply forget the payments for a longer period of time—say, a year or more—until he got back on his feet.

The representatives conferred and said they'd get back to him. The next week he was given official notice that the foreclosure proceedings had started. Mike began to look for another place to live.

A month later Bill called back. He wanted to know if Mike had any nibbles on the house. He hadn't. Bill also wanted to know how Mike's job hunting was progressing. Also no luck, Mike reported.

By the end of the next month, Mike and Jill made arrangements to move to her family's home in another state. They both hoped to get a better start there. Mike called the lender one last time and asked for a conference.

When Bill met with him, Mike pointed out that there was no way he could make up the back payments, now totaling nearly 11 months. Further, since the house was worth perhaps $15,000 less than the mortgage amount (if a buyer could be found at any price in this market), there was no way he could sell.

However, it would be 2 more months before the lender could complete foreclosure. Further, Mike had maintained the house well during that time and it was in great condition right now. However, if the lender persisted in seeking foreclosure, Mike would simply "walk." Chances are the house would be vandalized, and it might cost the lenders many thousands to put it back in shape. Also, there was always the cost of completing the foreclosure process.

However, if the lender would accept a *deed in lieu of foreclosure*—title to the property without going through the foreclosure process—Mike would transfer the property to the lender immediately. Then the lender could try selling the property itself, perhaps with more luck, since it might offer much better terms (financing) than Mike could. For Mike it meant that no record of foreclosure would appear on his credit report.

The lender's representative, Bill, considered and said he'd get back to Mike. He did the next day and agreed. A "deed in lieu" was drawn up and Mike was out from under.

A Deed in Lieu

While offering a deed in lieu is much better, from a credit perspective, than having a foreclosure on the records, it's still not wonderful. Mike's credit still noted months of nonpayment. And today many mortgage applications ask if a would-be borrower has ever given a deed in lieu. An answer of yes might still mean no new mortgage. However, a yes accompanied by a letter of explanation plus several years of good credit might indeed secure a new loan—*because there was no foreclosure on the record.* In short, foreclosure is the worst possible way to lose a house. A deed in lieu shows that the borrower made an effort to protect his or her credit. It's far, far better than foreclosure.

The Key to Negotiating Out of Foreclosure

The one most important point to understand in this example is that Mike and Jill constantly communicated with the lender. Communication was the key to their ability to get payments delayed and then get an alternative to foreclosure.

Consider that if Mike had never called the lender—had simply ignored the lender's calls to him (which, unfortunately, is what most borrowers in default do)—the lender would have simply written Mike and Jill off as a lost cause. It would have immediately started foreclosure and pursued that path to the end. In other words, the lender would have seen no alternative but to take the harshest possible course of action. Mike carefully presented the lender with a better alternative.

Lenders don't want to foreclose on homes. As we've seen elsewhere in this book, once a lender takes a property back, it becomes an REO (real estate owned), a liability instead of an asset. A lender would much rather give the borrower every opportunity to hang on to the house, or to get out from under by selling.

But when a lender sees that foreclosure is inevitable, it would much rather have a cooperative borrower who returns a home at minimal cost (the costs of foreclosure) in perfect shape than go through the procedure and then have to spend many thousands more refurbishing the home. (I have seen homes let go to foreclosure that were utterly destroyed inside and out, costing lenders tens of thousands of dollars to rehabilitate.)

What You Can Negotiate from a Lender

Lenders may be willing to do one or more of the following:

- Restructure the mortgage by extending the term so that you have lower payments, as long as the lender does not ultimately lose any interest.

- Temporarily allow you to miss payments until you get back on your feet by adding interest not paid onto the loan amount.

- Completely forgive interest and payments for up to a year or more, as long as you can demonstrate you have the potential to once again pick up payments after that time.

- Take back the property in lieu of foreclosure so that your credit report does not have a foreclosure showing up on it.

Tip

A big question is whether or not the loan is conforming. Remember, a conforming loan must meet the underwriter's parameters, the underwriter usually being a quasi-government secondary market lender such as Freddie Mac or Ginnie Mae. Thus, when it comes to foreclosure, the lender is restricted in what it can offer a desperate borrower by the guidelines of the underwriter. However, these guidelines have been so liberalized in recent years that they are very close to the four-point description listed above. A portfolio lender—a bank or an S&L, for example, that made the loan out of its own funds—might be even more liberal.

Keep in Touch

When in foreclosure, in order to negotiate the best possible deal with the lender, you must do the following:

- Constantly keep in touch. Immediately reply to any calls or letters from the lender, no matter when they come. Never let calls go unanswered.

- Try to get out from under the mortgage by selling the property.

- Clearly show the lender that your financial condition is such that you have no way to make the payments. This could mean being willing to send the lender, at any moment, bank statements, unemployment records, or anything else demanded. You can't be too finicky about keeping your finances private when you're faced with foreclosure as a real possibility.

- Make suggestions to the lender about how you would like the matter handled. If you think a vacation from payments would help you get back on your feet, present that as an offer. Only have a good reason why you'd be in better financial condition later and know exactly how long that will be. If you realize that you can't get out, consider a deed in lieu of foreclosure.

What's important is to present yourself as doing everything possible to get out of the mortgage problem you're in. It's not that the lender is sympathetic to your position, although those in the lender's employment may surely be. It's that you have to make the lender see that you have no other alternatives and that what you're proposing is better for the lender than foreclosure.

Trap

Don't try the sympathy approach. Mortgage lenders don't cry and they really don't care about you. What they want are performing loans. Barring that, they want the cheapest, surest financial method of solving the problem you are presenting. Offer them a viable solution and chances are they'll take it.

If you try negotiating your way out of foreclosure and make a dedicated effort, you could be pleasantly surprised at the results.

12
Bargaining for Personal Property

In the Introduction to this book, I noted that sometimes buyer and seller will negotiate over more than just the house itself. A dining room chandelier, a refrigerator or stove, a washer and dryer, even children's outdoors swings may be up for grabs. I recently sold a home in which I had put an L-shaped bench into a small kitchen alcove. It fit perfectly and really did make the room attractive. However, it was a piece of furniture, not part of the house, and I properly informed the buyers of that fact.

The buyers, however, could not see themselves living in the home without my table and bench. So they wrote it into the offer. They wanted to buy my house *and* those items of furniture. They made it a deal point.

Quite frankly, I wasn't all that concerned about the furniture. It hadn't cost that much and I really didn't know where else I could put it. However, as long as the buyers wanted it and apparently wanted it badly, I was willing to negotiate. I happened to need extra time to move. So I offered to trade off. They could have the table and bench, but I got to stay an extra 10 days, after the deal closed, without paying rent. They said fine, which was just great for me, since rent for that piece of property for 10 days would have been several times the cost of a new table and bench!

Trap

It's not usually a good idea, from the buyer's perspective, to have a seller remain in the property after the close of escrow. However, there's nothing illegal or unethical about it and if it's a deal point, the buyer may accept it.

What Is Personal Property?

It's important to understand the distinction between real and personal property. *Real property* refers to the land and anything attached to the land—the house, fences, separate garage, sheds, and so forth. *Personal property* generally refers to anything that you can take with you—clothing, furniture, children's toys, computers, TVs, washers and dryers, refrigerators, and so forth.

There is also a gray area that is very important in real estate because it sometimes causes confusion and leads to bitter squabbles between buyer and seller. Consider the following true story:

Peter and Rita negotiated a successful offer on a home that was about 7 years old. What Peter and Rita really liked about the house, in addition to its location and layout, were the expensive wood blinds on all the windows. The blinds gave the house a rich, modern look that very much appealed to them. They also liked the built-in refrigerator and stove/oven in the kitchen.

The escrow did not seem unusual and the sale concluded within about 5 weeks. The buyers had not asked for a walk-through. (They were out of town at the time, and besides the sellers were extremely neat and tidy people, so Rita and Peter figured the house would be left in good shape.)

A few days after the close of escrow, when Peter and Rita walked into their new home, they were aghast. It was clean and neat as a pin. However, all the wooden blinds were gone—the sellers had taken them. In addition, the sellers had taken the built-in refrigerator and stove/oven.

It took the buyers milliseconds to get on the phone and contact the agent, a long-time friend of mine, who was likewise surprised. She contacted the sellers, who explained as follows:

They had left the screws and attachment assembly for the blinds. But the blinds themselves had not been in any way permanently attached to the house. So the sellers considered them personal property and took them. They were using them in their own new home.

Further, the so-called built-in kitchen appliances were simply sitting in wells in the counter. They too were not attached in any way, just held in place by weight. They were easily removed and simply unplugged from electric sockets located under the counter. The sellers likewise considered these items personal property, took them, and planned to use them later on in another house they hoped to build.

Rita and Peter were horrified and angry. They said that one of the major reasons they had bought the property was the blinds and the built-ins. They wanted them returned immediately.

When the agent conveyed the message, the sellers simply replied, "If you wanted our personal property included in the deal, you should have specified it in the sales agreement. Barring that, those items are our personal property and we're keeping them."

The buyers were outraged, the sellers self-righteous. It appeared that the whole thing was headed for court. However, the agent prevailed upon the sellers to be reasonable and the built-ins were returned. Then the agent paid for part of the cost of new blinds from his own pocket—an expensive lesson learned.

This true story occurred nearly 20 years ago, and it's unlikely that it would occur today. Modern sales agreements typically provide (or agents should write in) that included in the purchase are all wall, window, and floor coverings and built-ins. Further, there's the walk-through, originated in part just because of this situation. Thus, today it is unlikely that Peter and Rita would find themselves in this sort of predicament.

However, the story does illustrate some of the gray areas between personal and real property. Very often, it's simply hard to tell. For example, is a swing set in the backyard real or personal property? What about an area rug in the living room? Or a vise on a workbench in the garage?

In real estate the determination of gray areas often hinges on a variety of things, including method of attachment and intent. For example, if the swing set is secured by having it sunk into holes in the ground, then the attachment suggests permanence and it probably is real property. On the other hand, if the swing set is simply sitting on top of the ground, it suggests portability and it's probably personal property.

Similarly, an area rug simply laying on the floor is undoubtedly personal property. But if it's tacked down and removing the tacks will leave marks in the floor it's probably real property.

Trap

Sometimes you can inadvertently convert personal property to real. For example, you own your home and you buy an expensive vise and workbench which you nail into the wall of your garage. When you bought the vise and workbench, it was obviously personal property. However, by your method of attachment, you may have converted it to real property.

How Do You Get Personal Property Included in the Deal?

As a buyer, you may fall in love with a piece of personal property just as Rita and Peter did in our example. It could be a beautiful, bell-shaped glass chandelier in the dining room. Maybe it's a portable barbecue outside or a great child's gym set in a sandbox. It could be anything, including the seller's large-screen TV set, which fits just perfectly in the family room, or the hope chest which looks so good by the window in the master bedroom. It can even be the seller's silverware or water skis!

If you're interested in items of a truly personal nature, such as silverware, water skis, or even clothing, most of the time it's best to simply buy these separately outside of the real estate sale. The reason is that when lenders see such items included in a sales agreement, they may devalue the real property by an amount they feel the items are worth. In other words, mortgage lenders aren't in the business of financing personal property.

Tip

On the other hand, any item which could be considered necessary to the operation of the home, such as a built-in refrigerator or washer and dryer, usually will receive more liberal lender treatment.

If you as a buyer want certain personal property included in the deal, there are basically two approaches that you can take: subtle and direct. The subtle approach is to not let on to the seller how badly you want the item. Instead of "oohing" and "aahing" about curtains over the kitchen window, you can simply not mention them at all. Then, when you fill out the sales agreement, be sure that it states that all window coverings are included in the sale. Presumably that would take in the kitchen curtains and when the seller agrees to the deal as written, they're yours. (You can check for them on the final walk-through.)

On the other hand, sometimes the seller will designate certain items that fall into a gray area as personal property. For example, a wood-burning stove insert (one that fits inside an existing fireplace) is going to be taken by the seller and is nonnegotiable. Now you're going to have to deal directly with the issue.

Tip

Remember, the word *nonnegotiable* usually means that you can get it, but it will cost you something.

If you want a piece of personal property that the seller obviously intends to take away, you automatically make it a deal point. For example, you may include a statement in your sales agreement that says the wood-burning stove insert is to be included as part of the sale.

By drawing emphasis to the insert, you've made it a deal point. If the seller has already said that the insert is not included in the deal—or even has said nothing—he or she may refuse to let it go. The seller may accept your offer, but cross out and initial the paragraph that has to do with the insert. Now you're in full-blown negotiations.

If you've made the insert a deal point, it becomes a matter of "What will it take to get you to give up that damn stove?" Maybe the seller wants to be paid more and maybe, if you really want it, you'll agree. Or maybe the seller wants more time (as I did in negotiating over an L-shaped bench). Or maybe the issue is a better interest rate on a second mortgage that the seller is carrying back. Withholding the stove is just another way of trying to get it.

Your choices here are to trade off or to increase the pie. We've already discussed trading off. Increasing the pie means that you attempt to demonstrate to the seller why it's necessary to include the insert as part of the deal. Maybe the house is in a cold climate and all homes in the area come with some sort of wood-burning stove. It's accepted as a necessary item. You might point out that to not include the insert would actually lower the value of the property. You wouldn't buy a home in the area that didn't have one, and chances are neither would anyone else. That sort of logic may prevail with a reasonable seller.

How Do You Keep Personal Property Out of the Deal?

There's another perspective here and that's the view of the seller. Thus far, we've seen how a buyer might get a seller to throw in a piece of personal property. But how does a seller keep a buyer from demanding it?

The answer is really quite simple. Remove it before the property is put up for sale—or make it quite clear that something in the gray area is definitely personal property.

For example, not too long ago I sold a property in which I had installed a lovely, and expensive, porcelain-and-brass light fixture in the dining room. My wife and I had purchased the fixture on a vacation and it was a memento of our trip. We really wanted to keep it. Of course, we didn't want it enough to throw out a sale.

The real problem, however, was how to keep the light fixture from becoming a deal point, since I suspected any buyer coming through would likewise want it and would insist upon it. The answer was simple. I went to a hardware store and bought another attractive, but inexpensive light fixture and replaced the one we wanted to keep. Then I packed up the memento and put it out of sight.

Thus, when buyers came to the house, they saw only the new light fixture. There could be no issue raised over the old fixture—it simply was no longer in place.

Similarly, a friend of mine had a rather nice swing set installed in concrete in holes in his backyard. When it came time to sell, he wanted to take it with him to his next house. However, he had no place to store it in the meantime.

So he dug out the swing set, filled the holes, and then laid it down on the ground in the backyard. He didn't go out of his way to mention it to buyers. But because it was laying on top of the ground, not buried in it, it was obviously personal property and not real. After the house sold, he took it with him. The buyer actually did comment on the "missing swing set," but when it was pointed out that it was obviously personal property, the buyer did not pursue the matter.

Tip

Sometimes the best way to negotiate an issue is to remove it from the bargaining table before negotiations begin.

The Bottom Line

Anything, including personal property, is negotiable. As a buyer, you can often get an item of personal property included in a deal simply by asking for it. It may turn out that the seller really doesn't care much one way or another. Or you may have to trade off to get what you want or find good reasons for the seller, who doesn't want to part with an item, to include it in the deal.

13

Prevailing in an Appraisal Argument from Homes to Income Property

There are two times you're likely to get into an argument with an appraiser. The first and most common is when you're seeking a new mortgage—either a refinance or a purchase—and the appraiser says the property isn't worth what you want for it. The second is when you get your property tax bill and you want to challenge it. We'll cover each separately.

What Do You Do When the Lender's Appraiser Says No?

When the husband of one of my neighbors died, she decided that she quickly wanted to sell a vacation home that they had owned. She talked to a few brokers, got a feel for the market, and put it up for sale for $200,000. (It was, indeed, a very nice place on a river in the Sierra foothills of California.)

To be fully prepared, she called one of the largest lenders in the state and paid for a formal appraisal, so that she could tell any prospective buyer that she had a mortgage lined up on the property.

I happened to be there when the appraiser showed up. It was a nice, warm morning and we walked around the property talking about real estate. After he had duly measured the lot and the house and written up the details of the home, we talked price. He said that in his opinion the property was not worth more than $130,000, tops. He had run a search for "comparables" in the immediate area going back the previous year, and there hadn't been any recent sales. Therefore, he had gone to another development some 10 miles away and used it for comparison.

I pointed out to him that he was dealing here with recreational property. That meant that demand for it was sporadic. A year or two might go by with no sales, then there might be one or two dozen sales in a matter of months. Further, I pointed out that the development he had used for comparables was not near the river and the community was not nearly as desirable.

He pointed out that the houses were of a similar age, design, and size. That was good enough for him. Since, after all, it wasn't any of my business, I demurred from saying more.

My neighbor, however, came to see me shortly afterward and said how terrible the appraisal was. She needed a lender to offer an 80 percent loan of $200,000. On the basis of its appraisal, the large lender had offered an 80 percent loan of only $130,000. The loan amount was $56,000 too low to allow her to make the sale she wanted. Wasn't there anything she could do?

I suggested that she contact a different lender—specifically, a very small bank with only three branches in the area. I told her that since the bank was located nearby, it might be more aware of the true property values. She agreed.

The new lender sent out its appraiser. Again, I was at the house when the appraiser came by and I walked the property with her. I mentioned the previous appraiser and noted that he had used comps from a development some 10 miles away. I also pointed out that I thought they were invalid and suggested, instead, that the appraiser use comps, no matter how old, from the present area. She agreed and found several sales 18 months earlier, all above $200,000. She sent in her report and my neighbor got a good loan commitment, for the full 80 percent of asking price. (She eventually sold for full price.)

How Do You Challenge a Lender's Appraisal?

There are essentially two methods of challenging a lender's appraisal that you consider to be in error. The above example lists one: Go to a different lender, one that has some reason to see it your way, and get another appraisal.

Another approach is to get the original appraisal reevaluated. This method is usually adopted when the initial appraisal comes, not prior to the sale, but after buyer and seller have signed a sales agreement. In this case, the buyer has already gone out, found a lender, and paid upward of $300 for the appraisal.

Trap

Arguing with a lender over the amount of an appraisal is a futile effort. Lenders are basically paper pushers. They need a piece of paper to prove the borrower's income, another to verify credit, and yet another to state the value of the property. The reality of people's lives or even the world at large matters little to them. Just give them papers that contain the right information, and the loan goes through. But if the papers don't say the right things, lenders simply can't (or won't) act.

Getting the Appraisal Changed

If you receive a bad appraisal from a lender, you need to get it changed. As noted, arguing over the appraisal with the lender is futile. You need to reach the level of the appraiser. You need to get the lender to request a reappraisal.

Unfortunately, this is not always possible. Some lenders adamantly refuse to reappraise. In that case, you will need to be satisfied with a lower loan—or go elsewhere.

However, many lenders will request a reappraisal. To get them to do this, be prepared to go to the lending officer and argue that the original appraiser made a significant mistake such as appraising the wrong property, not considering recent sales in the area, or not even coming into the home or looking at the backyard. (A little begging might work too!)

If you get a reappraisal, it might cost you another fee. Of course, if you get a better appraised value, it could be worth it.

Unfortunately, many lenders request that a reappraisal be done by the original appraiser, which means that you start off behind the eight ball. (You can request a new appraiser and some lenders will go along with you.) Naturally, in order to preserve his or her reputation, the original appraiser is going to come out determined to prove that the original figures were right. (On the other hand, you might get lucky and have a different appraiser who has no ax to grind.)

Either way, you need to be prepared. Yes, it's a good idea to get the house cleaned, mow the lawn, cut the shrubs, and plant some new flowers near the pathway in. But all these items really don't amount to a hill of beans when it comes to appraisal. What counts is the size of the lot and house, the style, the general condition, and most of all comparables!

That means that you need to do some investigating before the appraiser arrives. Work with one or more agents to find all sales of comparable homes in your area. Sales within the past 6 months are the most relevant, but if these are unavailable, go back further. Pending sales of homes (if you can find out the prices) are less helpful, but are better than nothing. Get documentation of sales from a real estate agent (a printed list with an agent's office logo on top is usually enough). Also, take the time to go to each of the places and take a picture. It really is true that a picture is worth 1000 words. If the appraiser sees that the comparable looks just like your home, he or she is going to be hard-pressed to deny it as a comparable. Thus, when the appraiser arrives, you will be well armed.

Tip

Be sure you're there to meet the appraiser. If you let him or her do it alone, you'll probably get the same negative result.

I suggest you remember the first rule of negotiating—make sure it's business, not personal. Be nice to the appraiser; don't be offensive by mentioning what a miserable job the appraiser did on the first go-round (even though it may be true!).

If the appraiser wants to remeasure the house (as most will), go along and chitchat. But be sure you present your list of comparables, along with square footage, number of rooms, floor plan, location, style, and most important, sales price. Personally hand the list to the appraiser and, if possible, go over each sale.

Most appraisers are honest at heart, and if you've done your homework and were able to find comparables to justify your price, they will admit that they "may have overlooked something." If they accept your comparables, you're probably home free. If they don't, you can try complaining to the lender again but, as noted earlier, it probably won't do you much good.

Tip

Your documented complaint to the lender about an appraiser who refuses to change the price even when confronted with comparables won't do the appraiser any good either. Appraisers count on referrals from lenders, and lenders want to make loans. If the lender suspects an appraiser of making and then hiding a mistake, that appraiser could spend a lot of time searching for new business. Appraisers know this, and it's a great motivating force for them to correct an improper appraisal.

Trap

Because of the fall in value of most properties during the last recession, many lenders have told appraisers to be conservative. If the appraiser has a choice between two figures, it's often the lender that insists on using the lower figure. There's no fighting this kind of logic.

A final word needs to be said regarding the cost of an appraisal. Today it's running in the $200 to $300 range. A reappraisal, as noted above, might cost you a second fee with no guarantee of a better result. However, it might be possible to split the costs. Since the borrower or buyer normally pays for the initial appraisal, it would be reasonable to ask the seller to pay for a reappraisal. After all, it's the seller's property value which is now holding up the transaction.

How Do You Challenge a Property Tax Appraisal?

This is a rather different matter. Whenever you own real property, the state (or county acting for the state) appraises it for tax purposes. These appraisals are typically made when the property is first improved (a home built on it), when it's sold, and in some jurisdictions every so many years thereafter. (In California under Proposition 13, the state can reevaluate the property only upon construction and sale.)

Rather than hiring an independent appraiser, the assessor's office often sends out a county employee to determine the value of your home for tax purposes. The method of appraisal is identical to that for a lender's appraisal. The size, condition, and (most of all) comparables are considered.

Be there, prepared, when the appraiser from the assessor's office shows up. County employees have a lot of property to assess and they don't like challenges to their appraisals, which slow down their work. Provide the appraiser with good, solid reasons that your property is worth only as much as you think (using comparables to back yourself up). Sometimes, just to avoid a challenge later on, the appraiser may simply go along.

Once the appraisal has been made, it is filed with the county assessor's office, and in due time (often several months) you will receive a notice telling you what the county feels your property is worth. The note may also give you a time and place for appealing the amount, although that's not always the case. (You can, however, always appeal, provided you meet usually very strict time deadlines.)

Watch Out for "Low" Appraisals

Some people receive their assessed valuation and are thrilled because it is so low—sometimes only half or a quarter of what they think the property is worth. Don't be fooled; you're dealing with politicians. There's also the "tax rate." This is the amount of tax you pay on your valuation. Politicians can agree to value property at half or a quarter of its true market value, then raise the tax rate to get more money. Most people look only at the valuation and don't pay attention to the rate.

Find out at what percentage of market value your house has been valued. (Call the assessor's office.) If it's half, then double the valuation figure to get how much the appraiser figured your house was worth. You could be unpleasantly surprised!

You will be given a time and place to appeal an assessed valuation of your property. Before you appear, go to the county assessor's office and ask to see the file on your property. (Don't be surprised to find it's only a 3" × 5" card. If it's a computer file, get a printout.) Check it carefully.

Be at the appeals hearing on time and be prepared. Don't argue emotionally (remember Rule 1); negotiate with facts. Here are some of the solid reasons that you can use to get an appeals board to change the valuation on your property:

Wrong comparables. Bring your own set of comparables with photos and a description that includes size and price. Have the list signed by someone knowledgeable about local property, such as a real estate agent.

Wrong description. Assessors make mistakes. Maybe they said your house had four bedrooms, when it has only three.

Wrong calculations. Did the assessor get the right number of square feet for the house? What about for the lot? Remember, assessors are only human and most are severely overworked. Mistakes of these kinds, unfortunately, are more common than people suspect.

Wrong exemptions. Different exemptions are available for homeowners, for religious property, and so on. Make sure you get the right exemptions—and all the ones you are entitled to.

Wrong extenuating factors.   Sometimes the assessor may miss
a detracting feature that reduces value to your property. For
example, if the property is next to a toxic waste dump, it's
likely to be worth significantly less than a comparable located
a mile away. Similarly, the assessor might overlook a utility
easement running through your front lawn that could lower
the value of the property.

How Do You Appeal an Improvement?

One last area that needs to be covered is making improvements
to your property—for example, by adding a new room or
putting on a new roof. Generally speaking, most counties will
reevaluate your property at that time and often will significantly increase its value.

Again, appeal—first to the appraiser in person and then, if
necessary, to the appeals board. It's very helpful to bring along
all the receipts for what the improvement cost. Any appraiser is
going to be hard put to argue that your new room addition
added $10,000 to the value of your property when you can
prove it cost only $5000. (But many appraisers will make the
argument that the new room added more to the value than simply its cost. Now, usually, the argument turns to comparables.)

Trap

Be careful of improving more than 50 percent of your property.
In many jurisdictions, when you improve more than half the
value, the entire property can be reevaluated. If you have an
existing low evaluation, it can now shoot up to current market
values. If you keep the improvement to less than 50 percent, frequently only the part improved can be reassessed.

14
Dealing in Investment Property

Most of the rules of real estate negotiation apply regardless of the type or size of the property. For example, you still want to aim for the moral high ground (Rule 4) and you want to keep the negotiation on a business level (Rule 1) whether it involves a small home, a strip shopping center, or a huge apartment complex.

However, when you get into investment property of one type or another, there are some additional deal points that need to be considered.

How Do You Handle Deal Points?

A deal point is simply something negotiable on which the deal hinges. In a home sale, it might be the price or the time for occupancy. In investment property, it could be a variety of sophisticated concepts ranging from gross income multiplier to capitalization rate to internal rate of return (cash on cash). Some of these concepts are too complicated to detail in this book, but the art of negotiating them remains virtually the same. And that's what we'll deal with in this chapter.

How Do You Determine the Price of Income Property?

There are many different methods of determining the value of an investment property. These include capitalizing the income of the property and determining the return on the actual cash invested. However, the most commonly used "quick method" for valuing real estate income property is the gross income multiplier.

For example, Sam owns a 23-unit apartment building. His total rental income is $11,500 a month, or $138,000 annually. What's the value of Sam's building?

Sam may tell you that the gross income multiplier for his area is 10.5. Therefore, his property is worth $1,449,000. How did he arrive at this figure? He simply multiplied the gross annual income by 10.5 ($138,000 × 10.5). That's the value, according to Sam.

Trap

Beware: The multiplier does not take into account the cost of borrowing money. Depending on interest rates and the amount financed, you may or may not be able to afford an income property regardless of what the multiplier says it's worth.

When the gross income multiplier is calculated, a percentage of the gross annual income, sometimes 5 percent, is usually deducted for vacancies. (We've not taken this into account for the purposes of our calculations here.)

Finding the Correct Multiplier

What should be apparent is that the value of any property is going to be determined in large part by that multiplier. The question: How did Sam arrive at a figure of 10.5? The amount of the gross annual multiplier, therefore, becomes a deal point.

The multiplier is strictly a rule-of-thumb method. There is no gross income multiplier fixed in stone. It's what anybody thinks it is. Having said that, let me further say that the idea of a multiplier is a bit more scientific than I've made out and, properly used, can be quite helpful.

Actually, the multiplier is found by, once again, looking at comparables. Consider the most recent sales of half a dozen comparable income properties. Divide the actual sales price of each by its gross annual income and you have a multiplier. Take the average of all six multipliers and you have a fairly accurate number to apply to your property.

If computed as indicated above, the multiplier can be a very useful tool. In fact, I've found that it is extraordinarily accurate, as confirmed by other methods. Of course, negotiations revolve around just how comparable other properties are and just what the current property's true gross annual income is.

Research Counts

Many owners and buyers, unfortunately, don't do a thorough job of researching comparables to come up with a true multiplier. Rather, they call up a few real estate agents and ask, "What's the income multiplier in this area?" The agent, who may or may not know anything about multipliers, might say 7, or 11, or whatever. Suddenly the number takes on mythic proportions and the buyer won't pay more, or the seller accept less. Don't accept anyone else's word for the multiplier until you see it documented with comparables.

Trap

Beware of "historic" multipliers. Sometimes an area will explode in value and multipliers will jump up. However, a year or so later when the explosion is over, those multipliers may settle back down. Except that sellers may still refer to the old numbers. Make sure that whatever multiplier you use is current with the times.

How Do You Find Out the True Rents?

Taking a giant step backward, what should be obvious is that the multiplier depends on two things: recent sales prices and the current rent from the property in question. While accurate recent sales prices of comparables should be fairly easy to obtain (call a few agents who deal in income property), determining the true gross income from rents for a specific property can be a bit tricky.

Pam was interested in buying a 7-unit apartment building. The owner was using a multiplier of 6, which was conservative for the area. The owner said all 7 units were filled, each was rented out for $450, and the gross annual income was $37,800 (7 × 12 × $450). With a multiplier of 6, that meant the building was worth $226,800.

Pam felt that was a reasonable price and bought. However, the first month she discovered that three of the tenants were months behind in their rent and a fourth, a brother-in-law of the owner, was living there free. By the time she kicked all the deadbeats out and rerented, Pam found her average monthly rental brought in only $350. For 7 rentals that was only $29,400 annually. When the multiplier of 6 was used, the true value of the property was only $176,400—$50,400 less than she paid!

Pam's story, unfortunately, is true more often than most people realize. Owners know that the way to inflate value is to get rents up artificially however they can. Too often, however, buyers find out the hard way that this has been done.

The true gross annual rental, therefore, like the gross income multiplier, is another deal point. Some investors I know use their own rule of thumb here. When a seller tells them the gross annual rental is one figure, they simply discount that figure by 10 or even 15 percent, then negotiate from there. To investors, this is the "puff factor." The owner is puffing up the rents to make the property appear more valuable than it really is.

A better way of dealing with the problem, however, is to get a true reading of the rents. This can be accomplished in several ways. A buyer can examine the cash receipts of the seller for the year. Or look at the rental agreements with the tenants. Or, if necessary, contact each tenant individually before concluding the sale to determine how much rent is paid and how current the tenant's payments actually are.

How Do You Deal with Deposits?

Deposits, the cleaning and security kind that tenants give to landlords to hold during the tenancy, may seem like small potatoes. But in recent years they have become increasingly important. In fact, in some cases they are the deal point around which a sale hinges. How can this be? It's all a matter of cash.

There's a very old joke that goes something like this. Sal says to Pete: "I've got good news and I've got bad. Which do you want to hear first?"

"What's the good news?" asks Pete.

Sal replies, "They've accepted our million-dollar offer for the office building."

"Great," Pete says and then asks, "So what's the bad news?"

"They want $500 in cash down!"

The truth of the matter is that most investment property deals are heavily financed. The buyer frequently has little cash money to put into the deal. But there is always a lot of need for cash—to pay off the agent, the closing costs, and the seller.

In an income property transaction, except for new financing, the only real cash in the deal may come from security and cleaning deposits. Consider: There's a 25-unit apartment building. Rents are $500 a month, making the price roughly $900,000 (assuming a multiplier of 6). That's a fairly large number even these days. But it's not a cash number. Presumably, the buyer is going to finance most of it, perhaps all of it, with the seller carrying back a substantial amount of paper. Except for the deposits.

Let's say that each apartment puts up one and a half times a month's rent in a cleaning and security deposit. (Currently that's the maximum allowed in some states.) That totals $18,750 ($750 × 25).

Often the owner has simply spent this money as it comes in (hoping to pay back a departing tenant with the deposit from the next tenant). Now negotiations deal with how to credit that money to the buyer. Sometimes the seller has carefully kept that money in a bank account. In this case, negotiations center on whether the seller gets to keep it or whether it's transferred to the buyer.

Since the deposits may be a significant part of the cash involved in the sale, they are a big deal point. Very often trade-offs in terms of price and financing can be made with them.

How Do You Deal with Financing?

The final deal point we'll consider is the financing. It's important to remember that the very best financing in the real estate world goes to owner-occupants of single-family homes. When you work with an investment property, the financing is less readily available and usually has a higher price.

For example, if you're buying an apartment building, a strip shopping center, or an industrial complex, you can forget about financing on the order of 80 percent of appraised value. (You may, however, get up to 80 percent from the lender that handled the construction loan. Such a lender will often offer good "take-out" or permanent financing in order to ensure that a buyer is found for the property.)

Good financing on investment properties will often be only 60 to 75 percent of market value, at a variety of interest rates. Thus, if a seller can offer good financing on a project by, for example, carrying back 20 or 30 percent in the form of a second (or third, fourth, or higher) mortgage, the trade-off can often be a higher price. Similarly, a buyer who comes in with a lot of cash can often command a much lower price.

Because financing is far more critical in industrial, income, and commercial property than it is in residential property, good financing commands far more leverage as a deal point.

The Bottom Line

As I said at the beginning of this chapter, the rules of real estate negotiation are basically the same for any size or type of property. The only things that are different for investment property are the deal points and the amounts involved.

15

Winning the Battle at Closing

During the course of most deals, you will find that at certain times you hold high leverage and at other times, low leverage. The clearest example I can give for this is a publishing contract to write a book. Most such contracts specify that an advance of some sort will be paid to the author. Usually half the money is paid upon signing and the other half upon delivery of a manuscript acceptable to the publisher.

At first the author has the higher leverage because he or she has the money, yet hasn't done any of the work. Were the author simply to take the money and run, the publisher would have a dandy time catching that author and getting the money back.

On the other hand, after the author goes to the trouble of writing the book and turns in the final manuscript, the shoe is on the other foot. Now all the work has been done, yet it's up to the publisher to accept and pay the author the second half of the advance—or to reject the manuscript. (If it's rejected, the author must, presumably, pay back the first half of the advance!) Now it's the author's turn to sweat because the publisher has the higher leverage. If the publisher wanted to, it could make all sorts of demands on the author, who would have to comply by rewriting, sometimes the entire book, in order to save the contract and get the remainder of the money.

In real estate, it's a similar situation with regard to the full course of completing a transaction. At the beginning, the buyers (and the sellers) have the high cards. They can negotiate price, terms, and all conditions from a position of high leverage— namely, if they don't like the deal, they can walk away from it with little to lose in terms of time (see Rule 18) and effort.

On the other hand, after an escrow has been run, a loan secured, the title cleared, and all documents prepared, it's time to close the deal and the shoe is on the other foot. Now when the buyers (or sellers) come in on the final day to sign the final documents, they have very little leverage. Yes, of course, if they don't like what's presented to them, they can walk away. But there could be severe penalties for doing so—not just the loss of the deal but also a possible demand for damages from the other party.

In this chapter we're going to consider the closing: the time when it's presumably too late to do anything but sign; the time when your leverage has ebbed to the lowest point.

What Can Go Wrong?

First off, let's consider some of the potential problems faced by the buyers at closing. It's at this time that buyers first see the actual loan documents they will sign. And sometimes (more often than professionals care to admit), the documents don't quite express the terms the buyers originally agreed to, or thought they did. Maybe there's an extra percentage of a point to pay, maybe the interest rate is a tiny bit higher, or maybe there's a list of extra garbage costs.

The RESPA Problem

The Real Estate Settlement Procedures Act (RESPA) is supposed to take care of such problems. As soon as you apply for a mortgage, the lender is required to issue you a preliminary statement telling you what your costs will be. This ensures that there won't be horrendous surprise changes at closing. If changes are necessary, a new statement must be issued.

But interest rates and points do fluctuate during the time a transaction is being consummated. And sometimes buyers just don't pay attention to all those extra costs mentioned in the preliminary statement. Or, infrequently, not all those little costs are included. In short, while RESPA has helped avoid the huge surprises previously sprung on buyers at closing, many small surprises still do slip through.

From a seller's perspective, the closing can also be a shock. Maybe the seller never did carefully add up all the costs that were going to come out of the sale of the property. These can include real estate agent's commission, payoff of existing financing, proration of taxes and insurance, termite inspection and repair, document fees, title and escrow charges, and maybe a dozen others. Sometimes happy sellers waltz into the escrow office only to have their day ruined when they realize that the amount they actually will receive from the sale is significantly less than what they had anticipated.

What Can You Do to Avoid Closing Problems?

A lot of problems can be avoided simply by anticipation. For the buyer, it's important to carefully read the RESPA statement and question any costs at the time you learn of them. That's when the closing process is just beginning and there's still time to switch lenders. Also, get in writing the actual loan commitment in terms of interest rate, points, and costs. If you're dealing with a reputable lender such as a big bank, an S&L, or a mortgage broker, the company will often stand behind any "mistakes" or low quotes that one of its employees made. But only if you've got it in writing.

If you wait until closing and have a problem with a lender, you basically have no leverage at all. You can yell, scream, and holler that you'll complain to the Federal Trade Commission and the state real estate licensing department. Even if these agencies receive enough complaints against an individual lender to investigate, their action probably will come months or years too late to help you. Usually your best approach is to be pleasant and try to negotiate small "misunderstandings." Sometimes responsible lenders will take out unnecessary charges.

Or you can pay. Usually it's simply too late in the deal to get a new lender, although sometimes this, too, may be possible depending on how long you have to close.

Additionally, it's helpful if buyer and seller keep in constant contact with each other (through agents, if necessary) so no surprises slip in at the closing. Each party should be issued a "preliminary closing statement" by the escrow holder or title company handling the closing, and it should list all anticipated costs. Read the statement carefully before signing and you can avoid a great many awkward closing situations.

From the seller's perspective, make sure you are aware of the true costs of all items you'll have to pay for out of the sale. You should be able to calculate this down to within a couple of dollars well in advance of closing and thus avoid any nasty surprises.

Tip

Any real estate agent worth his or her salt will prepare a list of costs and present it to the buyer or seller before the sales agreement is signed. I've seen agents who can present such lists down to within $25 of eventual costs. It's a service that good agents supply as part of their commission fee.

What Do You Do When Things Go Wrong?

Okay, we've discussed what to do to prevent problems. But what do you do if either you didn't pay any attention early on or something unexpected came up? You walk in to sign the final closing documents and the amount you'll receive is too low or the loan is wrong or there's some other condition that isn't quite right. What can you do about it at this late date?

The answer depends to a large extent on how gutsy a negotiator you are and who can correct the problem. If it's an issue between buyer and seller (not the lender or some other third party), then you actually may have more leverage than you realize.

In most cases (but not all!), by the time the deal is ready to close, both buyer and seller are most eager to get things over with. The buyer wants to get the property, the seller wants to get the money, and both have already made moving plans and told friends, relatives, and associates about the deal. To not go through with the sale now can mean financial as well as emotional distress. In other words, both parties want to make it happen.

Thus, when a buyer or a seller balks at signing the closing documents because of something unexpected in them, the other party is greatly upset—and may be willing to move mountains to get the deal closed. For example, the seller walks in, looks at the closing documents, and says in a surprised tone, "I'm being charged $1700 to prorate the taxes on this property. I was distinctly told at the time we signed the sales agreement that my cost wouldn't be more than $1000. It's $700 too high."

The escrow officer (or attorney or whoever is handling the closing) nods sympathetically and says, "You agreed to your prorations when you signed the preliminary escrow documents and the sales agreement. That's the amount you have to pay."

The seller says, "Nope. I refuse. I'll pay $1000 and not a penny more. Redraw the documents!"

Now the escrow officer is in a bind. He or she can't change anything unless both parties agree. So the escrow officer gets on the phone and calls the agent (if there is one), who calls the buyer and explains the problem. The agent says, "That crazy (see Rule 6) seller won't sign because of prorations and is threatening to walk out of the deal over $700." The buyer is irate, maybe even threatens to sue. The agent explains that the buyer's right, but then the deal won't close, the buyer won't get the house (at least not right away), and any lawsuit could take years—all over $700. An angry buyer eventually says, "Okay, give that lunatic the money—anything to close the deal."

Sometimes a party to a transaction will be sneaky and will use the closing to get something it otherwise couldn't get. Once, for example, I saw a buyer who wanted to get a rather spectacular front porch light included in the sale. (For getting personal property thrown in with the real property, see Chapter 12.) The sellers refused, saying it had cost them several hundred dollars. They were willing to sell it, but not just give it away. The buyer persisted for awhile, but in the end signed the sales agreement sans the lamp.

Then, at closing, the buyer refused to sign, saying she simply couldn't have the house without the front porch lamp. She wouldn't go through with the deal unless the sellers threw it in. You think the sellers were going to lose a sale on the day the deal was to close because of a porch lamp?

Trap

Beware of threatening to pull out of a transaction at the close. By then contingencies will have presumably been removed, which means that there may be no legally acceptable reason for you to back out. Your risk is that the other party will be sufficiently angry to refuse to back down and the whole matter could end up in court—where you could lose! On the other hand, most people will give in when there's a small amount involved, just to get the deal over with.

Who Controls the Escrow?

It's important to understand the true function of the escrow officer. (It doesn't matter whether a company or an individual such as an attorney acts as the escrow officer.) The person who opens the escrow, who sets it up, basically controls it. Why is this role important?

It's important because of the many functions the escrow performs. The escrow officer often is the one who calls to let you know some action required by the contract hasn't been completed. If the officer is lax in calling, the escrow can be delayed by days or even weeks.

The escrow officer is the one who calls for necessary documents. If the documents are called for too early, they may need to be redrawn, causing delays.

In short, the escrow officer can make the deal go smoothly or can make it drag out. How the process is handled is in part determined by the loyalty of the escrow officer. You want an officer loyal to you.

Who Pays the Escrow Fees?

There are usually two separate big extra charges at closing. One is for title insurance; the other is for the escrow. These fees are determined by the title insurance company and the escrow company.

Tip

Fees vary somewhat. Shop around to find the lowest. Also, if the property was sold in the recent past—say, in the last 2 years— there may be a big cut in the fees, *if* you ask for it.

Typically, how these fees are paid is determined according to the region in which you live. In some areas, they are split. In others, the buyer pays one and the seller pays the other. In yet others, the buyer or seller pays both—according to tradition.

I have nothing against tradition, but business is business and the payment of the escrow fees is negotiable. But if you want the other party to pay, make sure to make it a deal point at the time of negotiating the sales agreement. It's a bit late to do so when escrow is ready to close, although you can force the issue at any time.

Winning the battle at closing is 50 percent *chutzpah* (incredible nerve), 50 percent adequate preparation, and 100 percent luck. Be careful!

Appendix 1

The 20 Rules of Negotiating

There are four areas you must deal with when negotiating real estate. They are:

- PEOPLE (How to handle those with whom you deal)
- TACTICS (maneuvers that gain an advantage)
- STRATEGY (Having a good plan)
- TIME (Getting it on your side)

There are 20 rules:

RULE 1—Never Offend the Buyer or Seller

RULE 2—Beware of Choosing "Nice" People to Represent You

RULE 3—Never Believe Anyone Else Is Entirely on Your Side

RULE 4—Always Strive for the High Moral Ground

RULE 5—Disarm a Psychological Attack by Drawing Attention to It

RULE 6—Be Irrational, Occasionally

RULE 7—Strive to Be Innocent

RULE 8—Always Ask "Why?"

RULE 9—Question Authority

RULE 10—Challenge the Written Word

RULE 11—Listen Carefully

RULE 12—Always Give Yourself an Alternative

RULE 13—Be Informed

RULE 14—Work Only on Issues That Can Be Resolved

RULE 15—Never Respond to an Offer That Can't Be Closed

RULE 16—Don't Stick to the "Pie" Analogy or "Bottom Line" Reasoning

RULE 17—Remember That Some Deals Can't Be Made, No Matter What

RULE 18—Get the Other Party to Invest Time

RULE 19—Set a Deadline

RULE 20—Act Quickly

Appendix 2
Negotiating Without an Agent

If you're a good negotiator, you may want to change the typical format of handling a real estate negotiation. Normally, the buyer or seller uses the real estate agent as the negotiator, the intermediary. I'm suggesting that you may want to negotiate directly, yourself. This is not to criticize agents, most of whom do a good job.

Use the Broker or Go Direct?

Before I get thrashed by some old-time real estate agents who know the value of the broker/principal relationship, let me qualify the above statement. I have long maintained that the average person is far better off letting the real estate agent handle negotiations than trying to make the deal directly. That's because the average person is not skilled at negotiating a deal. Discussion can quickly degenerate into confrontation. People can take things personally and knock their heads together. The deal can easily go out the window.

However, the assumption that the buyer or seller (or both) is never a skilled negotiator, and that the real estate agent always is, is not necessarily true.

Not all agents are good negotiators. Some make a handsome living simply by listing property and hoping that others will close the deal for them. Other agents simply muddle through the negotiations, letting their buyer or seller down by not nego-tiating strongly. Just because you like an agent—and he or she does well at showing you properties or at gaining your confi-dence in listing—does not mean that agent will be able to do a good job for you at the negotiating table.

You may be more skilled at negotiations, particularly after reading this book, than your agent. In that case, I suggest you could do a better job by dealing directly with the buyer or seller, rather than letting the agent do the negotiating for you.

I'm not saying you shouldn't use an agent in a real estate deal. The agent's principal duty is to find a buyer for a seller. If an agent finds someone willing to buy your property (or finds a property you want, if you're a buyer) and you handle the nego-tiations to close the deal, the agent, in my opinion, is still enti-tled to a commission.

However, if you feel that you're a skilled negotiator (chances are you won't feel that way unless you've had some successes in negotiating), then I believe you should present the offer directly to the seller (or come to the buyer with your counteroffer). I realize this flies in the face of conventional wisdom, but then again think of your goal: Are you interested in justifying con-vention or landing the deal?

In real estate, negotiations for perhaps 90 percent of all resi-dential sales are handled by brokers. But not all. Some of the more spectacular deals have been struck by the buyer and seller working face to face, provided at least one of them is a skilled negotiator.

What If the Agent Throws Up a Roadblock?

Occasionally if you're a buyer, your agent may say that you can't present the offer directly to the seller, that the seller has specified that only the broker can present the offer. (Similarly, the buyer's agent may make an appeal that only he or she can present a counteroffer to the seller.)

That's a lot of hooey. Most times the seller or buyer doesn't care who presents the offer. The agent's just trying to protect the deal (making the assumption that you'll blow it) or is afraid of losing a commission.

If you demand to present the offer, I don't see how an agent can stop you. If the other party has indeed requested that only an agent present the deal, then you can agree to have the other party's agent present, sort of as protection. If the seller absolutely refuses to see you, you can make this offer: "I will buy your house. But you must deal with me directly." If you put up $5000 as an earnest-money deposit along with a signed offer, I can't imagine a seller not talking directly to you.

Whose Side Is Your Agent On?

I firmly believe that no one can serve two masters at the same time. No agent can faithfully serve both buyer and seller. If the agent represents the seller, he or she cannot fully represent the buyer—and vice versa. Yet many agents appear to do so.

Today, most states have strictly seller's agents and strictly buyer's agents. Some states have a confusing combination arrangement: The agent has both buyer and seller sign a statement saying that the agent represents them both, except not entirely and not in every situation.

Be sure you determine whom your agent works for. If you're a buyer and the agent is working for the seller, be careful of confiding your thoughts on price and terms to the agent. Your agent has a fiduciary responsibility to reveal your confidences to the seller! The same holds true if you're a seller talking to a buyer's agent. If the agent presumes to represent both parties, then probably neither party should confide.

Most buyers and sellers use agents as a kind of financial "dutch uncle" to try out price or terms they might consider. There's nothing wrong with this, as long as the agent is your fiduciary. Watch out, however, if the agent is working for the other party.

When an Agent Works Against You

Even if you're working with an agent who is presumably strictly on your side, there are still some subtle, even unconscious, conflicts of interest that can crop up. Remember that an agent works in a community, and it's to his or her advantage to see that every deal is a good deal for all concerned. The reason an agent wants things to work out this way is, simply put, *repeat business.* He or she wants to continue doing business in the community and seeks recommendations (the bread and butter for new clients). In short, the agent wants to maintain a reputation.

This desire for a "fair deal" every time has some interesting ramifications in negotiations—ramifications that are not always to your advantage. Let's say you're a buyer who, naturally, wants to get the lowest possible price on a house. (Obviously, this is the desire of every buyer.)

An agent shows you a suitable house and you decide you want to make an offer. Only you want to lowball it. The asking price is $175,000 and you want to offer $35,000 less than the seller is asking. You explain your offer to your agent and, further, state that you want to give the seller a 24-hour deadline to decide—no more. (See Rule 19.)

The agent balks at this and argues against it. She says that the offer is ridiculously low, the seller won't even consider it, and it's not worth presenting. Further, the short deadline is a bad idea. The agent argues that you can't "push people around like that." You have to be fair, give people time to consider. In short, she doesn't want to present your offer.

Now is the agent looking out for your best interests? Or her own? In some circumstances a lowball offer accompanied by a short deadline can be very effective. This is especially the case when the seller has had few or no other offers and is desperate to sell.

But if the agent doesn't want to take in the deal, I would suspect that part of the reason is that she doesn't want to get a reputation as someone who brings in lowball offers. It could affect the agent's ability to list other properties in the community. (Would you list with someone who brings you very low offers?)

She also doesn't want to get known, especially in a small town, as a high-pressure salesperson, someone who brings in offers with short fuses (deadlines) and thus "pushes people around."

She may truly feel you're making a bad offer. She says she wants the best deal for *both* you and the seller. But do you really care if it's the best deal for the seller? Or are you concerned about getting the best deal for you?

If you insist, and she's a conscientious agent, she may decline to work with you, the honorable way out. If she's not quite so conscientious, she may indeed take in the offer but then make only a halfhearted presentation, which will surely not get the sale. You could lose the purchase, not because of your offer, but because of your agent.

How can you count entirely on this agent? She may indeed want to do the best for you. But conflicting with that impulse may be her desire to maintain a reputation in the community among sellers and other agents. She certainly wants to go on to sell many more properties. For her, yours is only one deal out of many and it's the big picture she's looking at.

For you, however, it's a one-and-only deal. You'll probably never see this seller again. Most likely, you don't have a reputation as a real estate negotiator to worry about. (Indeed, the better a deal you make, the more respect you're likely to get from your peers.) Further, you can't count on making up on the next deal what you lose on this one. For you this is a "one shot" and it's to your advantage to get the best deal possible.

In short, your interests and those of your agent could be in conflict.

What is a good agent going to do in this situation? As noted, I've known excellent agents who, when faced with taking in an offer that they really don't want to present because of personal reasons, do the right thing and simply tell the buyer, "I'm sorry, but I really can't represent you. I think you'd be happier with some other agent." In other words, they realize that they can't act in the best interest of the buyer and bow out.

On the other hand, I've also known agents who continue to work with buyers (or sellers) no matter what, even when they aren't representing them faithfully. A good rule of thumb is, when your agent starts arguing that he or she doesn't want to present the offer you're ready to make, it's time to get a new agent.

There's a very fine line between advice that's in your interest and simple sales pressure. A good agent may indeed point out that it could be to your advantage to make an offer—to counter—and may even suggest a realistic price. On the other hand, a not-so-good agent may use a variety of arguments to bully or even scare you into making an offer that you really don't want to make.

If you ever find yourself negotiating with an agent over the kind of offer or counteroffer to make, you are being pressured. The agent should present alternatives, not insist on what's best for you. If the agent insists, it could be that he or she is really interested in what's best for the agent.

This advice is not to suggest that you should never trust your broker. It's only to point out that you should never put all your trust in any other person in a business transaction. (See Rule 3.)

Appendix **3**

Negotiating with
a Builder

Most people believe that it's impossible to negotiate with home builders. This is understandable, since the builders sometimes go to great lengths to create that impression.

For example, a typical builder may construct a few model homes for all potential buyers to walk through. The prices on the models are clearly marked. The most basic home—Model A, the "Hereford"—is priced at $103,000. Model B, the "Shetland," has a fourth bedroom and is $112,000. Model C, the deluxe "Country Estate," offers a spa in the master bedroom and is $124,995. Extras are available—hardwood cabinets, wall-to-ceiling mirrors on the master bedroom closet doors, and upgrades in carpeting and countertops—and are clearly marked as to cost. It's sort of like being in a department store. There's a price for everything and the implication is that nothing is negotiable.

Of course, nothing could be further from the truth. Everything with regard to a new home is negotiable. It's just that you have to make an extra effort to get to the negotiation table.

Knowing What You Want

Before we examine the actual negotiation process involved with buying direct from a builder, it's important to understand the basic rule when purchasing a new home: You can't get what you want until you first know what that is. When you buy a resale, you spend a great deal of time trying to find something existing that will fill your needs and desires. With a builder, by contrast, you can often get your wishes built to suit.

Now that doesn't mean that the builder is going to dramatically change all construction plans to accede to your every whim. But it often does mean that, if you get involved with a builder during the construction process, you can choose the color of the interior of the home or the quality of the carpeting, kitchen counters, and cabinets. Many times, you can also decide on a few design features such as whether a basement or attic is built out or left rough or whether a kitchen has recessed ceiling lights or a built-in window planter. In other words, whereas with a resale what you see is what you get, with new construction you have some flexibility.

Be forewarned, however. There's not as much flexibility as some people think. A speculative builder (one who builds first and hopes to find a buyer later) typically will have a set of basic plans which have been approved by the local building department and by lenders for a certain mortgage amount. Further, the builder knows, sometimes to the dollar, how much everything will cost in terms of labor and material. To vary from these basic plans would mean delays and potentially very high extra costs for the builder. Hence, it's unlikely that you'll get the builder to agree to change the basic layout of a home. The builder won't want to add a nook here or a bedroom there. You won't be converting a one-story to a two-story or the other way around. Yes, you can make minor changes, but very often not major ones. If the builder does agree, you can be sure it's going to cost you megabucks.

Tip

If you want to make changes that involve "design," you're probably better off buying a lot and then either hiring an architect and builder to create just what you want or doing the design and construction work yourself. But be prepared to pay more, lots more. Custom work always costs more than ready-built.

Making a List of What You Want

Before getting directly involved in negotiating with the builder, it's very useful to create a list of exactly what you want. Remember, you won't get it unless you know what it is.

Here's a partial list of items over which you would typically have some choice in new home constructions.

Indoors

Air conditioning (capacity, economy)

Appliances (quality, color)

Cabinets (material, quality, color)

Carpet (quality, color)

Carpet padding (quality)

Countertops (material, quality, color)

Doors (hollow or solid core, material, quality)

Finishings (railings, handles, light switches)

Flooring in entry, kitchen, bath (material, color)

Heater (capacity, economy)

Light fixtures (design, quality)

Mirrors (location, size, quality)

Paint (color, quality)

Plumbing fixtures—toilet, sink, and so on (quality, color)

Rough or finished extra rooms

Water heater (recovery rate, size)

Windows (quality, planter box)

Outdoors

Driveway (material, width)

Fencing (complete, partial, none)

Insulation (more)

Lot (location, size)

Roof (material, quality, color)

Walls (material, quality, color)

Yard (landscaped front or back, quality)

As you can see, there are many, many choices. It's a good idea to visit several developers' models to get an idea of what's being offered in your area. As you go, note those items which appeal to you; then add them to your list. When you finally come to the builder whose home you want to purchase, you should have a fairly complete idea of those items which you must have, those which you would like to have, and those which you can live without.

The "Upgrade" Trap

Builders, of course, understand exactly what you, as a buyer, are doing. They know that you are looking around at this model and that and are aware that you are making a list of your options. They know you are doing it and they are prepared for you. It would be hard not to find a builder of spec houses who didn't have his or her own list of "options" and "upgrades."

Options are design changes which the builder has anticipated buyers might want and for which he or she has already received building department and lender approval. The builder also knows their exact cost. You want a built-in love seat in the family room—no problem. He can put it in. You want a skylight in the master bedroom—no problem. You can have it. All for more money, of course.

Similarly, there are upgrades, or items the builder can change in terms of material, quality, and color. You want thicker carpet—again, no problem. You want granite countertops instead of tile—it can be handled. All for more money.

What should be obvious is that there are actually two issues here. The first is the breadth and depth of the builder's list of options and extras. The second is cost. We'll deal with each separately.

The Builder's List

As noted earlier, the builder usually must get approval for changes from the building department and the lender. Further, a good builder will have penciled in all the costs for labor and material for the basic plan as well as any options and upgrades.

The number of items and the variety offered will differ from builder to builder. A good builder, however, will have a lot of options and upgrades available. Typically, the higher-priced the home, the larger the list.

Arguing over the Builder's List

Although builders are normally quite willing to grant you any item on their list, at a price, they are extremely unhappy about adding something not on their list. Some strange arguments can result. For example, a friend of mine got into a paint feud with a builder. The builder had a series of colors from Sherwin-Williams, but the color my friend wanted was from Sears. For some reason, the builder just didn't have just the right shade on his list. My friend suggested that as a solution the builder get the paint from Sears, but the builder insisted it had to be from Sherwin-Williams. (*Note:* The roles of the two paint companies could just as easily be reversed. The point here is not that either has better paint or more colors. They both offer excellent products.) As it turned out, the builder was probably locked into a price and had already agreed to purchase a certain amount of paint. He or she never acceded to my friend's wishes.

Problems can occur with any option or upgrade. You want a particular brand of carpeting. The builder offers a different brand. For the same reasons, getting the builder to switch brands is going to be very tough.

In short, if what you have on your wish list coincides with what's on the builder's available options and upgrades list, your chances of being able to get it are excellent. On the other hand, whenever the two lists differ, you're in for a fight.

The Builder's Costs

The other part of this equation is the cost to you. This will often become most clear with regard to carpeting. Today many new homes offer wall-to-wall carpeting. However, often the padding is very light and the carpeting is of a low quality. Many home buyers want to upgrade both.

If you want to upgrade, the builder may smile and direct you to the "design center." This is usually a showroom, either at the development site or at a commercial store located off site. Here you will be shown a variety of colors, patterns, and qualities. The trouble is the price.

In my experience, the price at the builder's design center is often two or three times higher than what you could get for the same carpeting elsewhere on your own. It may quickly become evident that the builder has added a significant profit to the upgrades.

At this point, many would-be buyers will say something like, "We don't like your choice of carpeting. We'd prefer to get our own."

Fine, the builder may reply. "However, you'll have to get your own *after* you move in." In other words, you'll have to take up and discard the builder's carpeting to put in your own—a costly and wasteful procedure.

"No," you may protest. "We want to put our own carpet in place of yours—and since you won't be putting in any carpet, we'd like a credit."

At this the builder may snicker and say something like, "Not on your life!" The explanation may go something like this: In order to sell the property, the lender requires that it be completed and that includes all carpeting down and in place. The builder cannot sell the home and you cannot get a new mortgage without carpeting down.

This argument is usually very true. As a consequence, if you want to put your own carpeting in, it would have to be done *before* you buy. Serious complications can ensue. What happens, for example, if at the last minute you can't complete the transaction? Do you lose the money you paid for the carpeting? Does the builder need to pay you back? (Unlikely.) Further, if you buy the carpeting yourself and pay for it to be laid yourself, there is the question of mechanic's liens that the builder has to worry about. (If it turns out you have a disagreement with the carpet people and don't pay, will the builder be liable for the costs even after you buy?)

As you can see, there are many roadblocks that the builder can raise in front of you. It will seem so much easier simply to go to the design center and pay what may be outrageously high prices for upgrades or options.

Everything Is Negotiable

It doesn't have to be that way. Later in this appendix we'll look at specific negotiating techniques to use with builders. However, at this stage it's worth pointing out that all upgrades and options are negotiable. You can get them your way and often at your price.

In our example of carpeting, you could have the builder buy the carpeting you want and install it. There would be no problem with mechanic's liens that way. Further, you could give the builder a nonrefundable check to cover a large portion of the amount between your discount on the builder's carpeting and the cost of your choice. Of course, you would be at risk of losing your money if the deal didn't go through. But if you paid only a portion, the builder would be at some risk too, and would certainly want you to get the home. Also, you could get the carpeting laid at the last minute to reduce the risk of the deal not going through.

The point here is that where there's a will there's a way. And after some initial arguing, builders may be willing to comply, particularly in recent slow markets.

Market Leverage

This brings up another important point. How much leverage you have with a builder will often depend not so much on what you say as on the market conditions at the time. A decade ago builders across the country were putting up developments containing hundreds or even thousands of homes. They couldn't be bothered with the whims of individual buyers. If one buyer didn't want to pay full price, go along with the builder's terms, or fit into the options and upgrade list, there was always another buyer to take his or her place.

Then came the real estate recession. These very builders often were left holding hundreds or thousands of unsold homes. They bent over backward to sell. They gave interest rate buy-downs (discussed shortly) and threw in options and upgrades for free. Still they couldn't sell. A good many builders simply went bankrupt, with their properties sold off at auction.

The great sell-off of the last real estate recession was a wonderful time for home buyers. But those days are largely gone. Today, most builders and developers put together only a few dozen homes at a time. They are well financed and have priced the homes to sell in today's market. Typically they won't start building more until they have sold what they have.

Thus, if you're under the illusion that the builder is forced to accede to your demands because of market conditions, think it through again. The days of the hot property—when buyers would wait outside sleeping on cots to be the first to bid—are gone. But so are the days when builders were offering homes at fire-sale prices (at least in most parts of the country, as of this writing).

Today there are seasoned builders who know their costs, don't get overleveraged, and are tough negotiators. In short, builders tend to be lean and mean. That doesn't imply, however, that you can't successfully negotiate with them. It just suggests that you would be in error if you expected them to lie down at your feet and beg you to buy.

Getting Negotiations Started

Perhaps the hardest part of negotiating with a builder is getting the process started. Remember, the builder knows what you have in mind and in most cases has taken care to see that you are discouraged from negotiating.

As noted earlier, the various models are usually offered at set prices—sort of like the way different varieties of mayonnaise are priced in a grocery store. And there are set prices for upgrades and options. In many cases, there are specific mortgage packages already in place that you are encouraged to use. For example, you may be told that if you want to pay all cash (get your own financing), the builder will be happy to sell to you. Unfortunately, you will have to spend more money in appraisal and lending fees. It will simply be much easier to get the financing that the builder already has in place.

Further, the salesperson may say that he or she is authorized to accept only full-price offers, on the terms and conditions specifically written out. In other words, the implication is that nobody negotiates price, terms, and so on with builders. The agent may argue, "Don't you realize these are *new* properties and are worth what the builder says they're worth?"

Not so. When dealing with a builder, you can negotiate. The best approach is to submit a prepared offer. Do so either directly yourself or through an agent. If you use an agent, be aware that the builder may not be willing to pay an agent's fee and you may end up having to pay it yourself.

If you submit it yourself, I suggest that you write up an offer (using expert counsel, such as an attorney or competent agent) and deliver it to the builder's sales office. The representative there should be a licensed real estate agent and should know the rules of the game. Accompany your offer by a reasonable deposit (several thousand dollars) and tell the agent that you would like to submit it to the builder or owner.

The agent may be very pleasant, quickly agree to do so, and promise to get back to you as soon as possible. I suggest you tell the agent that you want to present your offer in person. After all, you should have some negotiating tricks up your sleeve after reading this book. Again, the salesperson may readily agree.

On the other hand, the salesperson may stonewall you. I once had a salesperson say that the builder absolutely refused to consider any offer that was not accompanied by a $10,000 cashier's check. The agent would not let me speak to the builder and refused to accept my offer. I was able, however, to get the name of the builder (it was blazoned in huge letters on a sign outside) and I called direct. I spoke first to a secretary, explaining that I had a cash offer (down payment plus financing on my end, cash to the builder). I was then connected directly to the builder, who invited me in. We eventually did not make a deal, but it wasn't because I couldn't get to the builder or owner or because he insisted on a ridiculous sort of deposit.

Trap

Beware of salespeople who are officious. Most real estate agents will go out of their way to be helpful and courteous. But I have encountered a few salespeople at development offices who seem to have an attitude problem. It's as though they feel put upon in having to work with you. If you encounter such people, I suggest you try an end run, as explained above.

What You Can Negotiate

With a builder you can negotiate price, terms, options, and extras. Read the appropriate chapters in the text for tips on negotiating price and terms. We've already covered a bit on extras and options. Here are a few additional points to consider.

Often an individual owner on a resale has more flexibility than a builder. An owner may have been in the house for years and built up a considerable equity. If you offer 20 percent less than the asking price, the owner may be willing to consider it.

However, builders usually work on much thinner margins. They may have only 10 or 15 percent into the property, after accounting for all costs (including the costs of holding inventory, as described below). Thus, if you offer 20 percent below asking price, the builder may not be able to comply with your offer even if he or she truly wants to.

On the other hand, as noted earlier, builders often have a huge markup on options and particularly upgrades. They can often be very flexible when negotiating these.

Tip

Sometimes you can find a development home that already has the upgrades and options put into it. Perhaps they were put in for an earlier buyer whose deal fell through. The builder will very likely be anxious to get rid of this home and may be very flexible when negotiating for those upgrades or options.

There's also the matter of holding costs. With an individual on a resale, you as a buyer often want to know how long the house has been on the market—under the often correct assumption that the longer the time, the more desperate the seller is to make a sale.

With a builder it's even more extreme. A builder must pay interest each month on unsold homes in inventory. Typically, speculative builders will have included an allowance for this— say, four to six months. If the homes get sold sooner, there's an additional profit. Even if it takes six months, there's no loss. Problems for these builders arise when their inventory sits around unsold for long periods of time. Their holding costs can eventually drive them into bankruptcy.

Therefore, your leverage increases the longer a fully con-structed home has been sitting around unsold. If it has been fin-ished for six months, you should have lots of leverage.

Tip

You can determine how long the house had been completed by going into the garage and finding the building permit sign-off sheet. Usually it is tacked to a wall and remains there until a buyer is found for the property. The sheet will contain dates and the signatures of building inspectors. Look for the word "final" and the sign-off date.

Mortgage Buy-Downs

In days of higher interest rates (as happens periodically), the reason builders can't sell their homes is that people can't qualify for mortgages. As an inducement to purchase, therefore, sometimes builders will offer *buy-downs.*

In a buy-down, the builder gives a certain amount of cash to a lender (buys down the purchaser's mortgage); in return, the lender offers the purchaser a lower interest rate. Typically, the lower rate varies. For example, it might be 3 percent lower than market the first year, 2 percent lower the second, 1 percent lower the third, and at market the fourth.

If you are a buyer, this reduction will lower your monthly payments, often significantly, and make it far easier for you to qualify for a loan. Indeed, you may be thinking that you're getting a real bargain here. What's important to keep in mind, however, is that there's no free meal in real estate. What is given away in one hand is often taken back in the other.

The builder may have increased the price of the home to offset the buy-down on the mortgage. For example, let's say it costs the builder $3000 in cash to buy your mortgage down. That builder may have increased the price of the home $3000 (or cut costs by that amount). Are you getting a bargain? Nope. You're getting a trade-off.

What I suggest is that you do *not* give a builder negotiating points for a buy-down. In most cases, you're getting nothing more than you would if you paid less for the property and got a higher interest rate.

There are lots of good reasons for buying brand-new homes. They tend to have fewer maintenance problems. The neighborhoods are often cleaner. Everyone is in the same boat (with a new house).

There are also some negatives. The new house may have lots of problems, and it can be a hassle to get the builder or the warranty company to fix them. Or the neighborhood may not develop as you hoped it would.

Good or bad, a new house does not have to be bought at a fixed price. Remember, you can negotiate price, terms, upgrades, and options.

Negotiating at Auction

Ever since the great real estate recession of the late 1980s and early 1990s, auctions have become a familiar method of disposing of real estate. As this book is being written, I am aware of at least two auctions of nearly 90 homes to be held nearby over the next weekend. It's very likely that auctions will continue to be a method of selling properties that, for one reason or another, cannot be sold by conventional means.

For the buyer, the allure of these auctions is the chance to purchase a home for a greatly reduced price. On the other hand, the danger is that the buyer will pay too much or get a property that has an unfixable defect. Most auction buyers with whom I've talked have been satisfied with their purchase. They feel they got a fair price. A few, however, later on felt they paid far too much.

The proper approach is to find out what's wrong with the property and why it isn't being sold conventionally. If the problem is temporary or can be fixed, it's possible to get a good buy. We'll look into all these considerations below.

Understanding Auctions

Auctions as a means of selling a commodity are not new. They are a tried-and-true method of selling, dating back to the bazaars of ancient Mesopotamia.

In an auction, ancient or modern, owners of commodities—whether they be jars of olive oil, gold coins, or real estate—consign their wares to an auctioneer. The auctioneer, a person skilled in dealing with crowds, assures the owners that he or she can sell their merchandise for them and get a good price for it. They trust the auctioneer. They put their faith in his or her hands.

Modern real estate auctions are frequently advertised through full-page ads in major newspapers. There also may be an expensive, colorful brochure describing the property. On the day of the auction, treats and champagne may be served to the bidders.

But don't be confused by the glamour and glitter. It's still the sale of a property. And if you're a buyer, you need to follow the same rules: Find out why the property is being auctioned, figure out the maximum you ought to pay, and don't pay too much.

The Reserve Auction

A *reserve* means that there is a minimum price below which the seller will refuse to sell. (Sometimes the reserve amount is not announced.)

In reality, most auctions are reserve sales. Few sellers are willing to take a chance that there will be a low turnout (and hence, only a few low bids) because of poor weather, competition from other auctions, or simple lack of interest. What this means, therefore, is that when you go to one of these auctions, you may not be able to get a "steal." The seller can reject any really low price as being below the reserve.

Of course, the seller doesn't have to honor the reserve. If it appears that there has been strong bidding on the property, but bidders really don't feel it's worth as much as the reserve, the seller may opt to take the highest bid below the reserve. I've seen this happen several times. Usually, however, it's not done right at the time of the auction. Rather, the seller contacts the highest bidder later and says, "If you'd still like to take the property at your highest bid, it's yours."

Watch out for auctions in which nothing is said about a reserve. In a straightforward reserve auction, the auctioneer will announce that there is a reserve and will state the minimum bid.

The Absolute Auction

Absolute auctions are much more popular with buyers, since they afford an opportunity to get a property for virtually nothing. *Absolute* means that there is no reserve. The highest bid takes the property, no matter how low that price may be. At a typical auction, the majority of properties will be "reserve," but a few will be sold "absolute."

You may get a better deal at an absolute auction. But just remember, you're not likely to be the only one who thinks so. There will probably be a lot of people out there hoping to get a steal, and together you could force the price up higher than it really should go. Sometimes absolute auctions get higher prices than reserve auctions!

The Draw of the Spectacle

As noted earlier, beware of all the hoopla that often surrounds an auction. It might be held in a beautiful white tent with balloons and streamers. The auctioneer and his or her associates may be dressed in tuxedos. The whole thing may have an upscale "event" beat to it. There may be free food and wine tasting. (It goes without saying that you should never drink intoxicating beverages while you're conducting real estate or any other kind of business!)

Don't be fooled. The atmosphere is carefully orchestrated to create a "group mentality," an outlook calculated to make you loosen your wallet and think that you're getting a great deal. It still all comes back to dollars and common sense. The auctioneers can put a washed face on it, but it's still a hard sell and you'd be wise to keep one hand on your wallet at all times.

The Auction Procedure

Most auctions require that you show up with a certain amount of cash or credit in order to bid. You may have to fill out a form and submit to a credit check. Or you may need a cashier's check for a set amount.

Once you bid and are successful, you will be expected to turn over that check immediately or to present cash or money in other form as a deposit. You will also be required to execute a sales agreement and apply for a mortgage, usually with a lender previously determined by the seller.

It's important to understand that if you win the auction and then don't complete the sale, you could lose your deposit. Further, the auction company usually doesn't want you to have any of those contingencies—opportunities to back out—that you might have with a conventional sale.

Also, when you buy at auction, you may not be able to let the sale hinge on having the property inspected; you're usually stuck with it once you win and execute the documents. When you get to the purchase agreement, you may find that you're asked to agree to all the terms the seller wants. Be sure that you read everything you sign carefully. If you're new to auctions, it's a good idea to have an attorney or a competent and experienced real estate agent present to help you.

You do have some recourse should things go sour. In almost all jurisdictions, real estate auctions are subject to state laws. If the deal doesn't work out as you had been told and you feel you are being cheated, you can contact your state's real estate licensing board.

Check the Property Out

The first step in negotiating at auction is to determine if you even want to play the game. Usually when a home is sold at auction, there's a problem with it. The problem may not be physical, as in the case of a fixer-upper. But it may still be tangible. Here are some typical problems.

1. *There's a terrible market with no buyers.* Perhaps the seller or builder has gone bankrupt, and the bank has foreclosed and is now the seller. The bank can't handle a big bunch of homes, so it has hired an auction firm to dispose of them.

Most buyers here hope and anticipate that they can get the home at a fire-sale price, live in it (or rent it) for a period of time until the market turns around, and then sell it for a whopping profit. Be aware, however, that this is less and less the case with real estate markets improving everywhere as we move into the late 1990s. Don't get caught thinking you're getting a depressed market bargain in a good market. If it appears that way, something may not be right and you'll most likely be the one to lose.

2. *The house is overpriced.* Sometimes builders goof and spend too much on houses for the area. I've seen builders put in $400,000 + homes in areas where the highest-priced resale is $250,000. No way is anybody going to pay full price for an overbuilt property.

There's no reason not to bid on a house in this situation, however, as long as you get it for the right price. That price should be no more than neighborhood comparables justify.

3. *The house is in a terrible location.* Sometimes builders find a marginal piece of land—say, near a freeway or a railroad track. The reason it's marginal is that nobody wants to live there. But it's cheap, so they buy the land and build. Naturally, once the homes are up, the builder can't find buyers.

I would stay away from this sort of property, unless the price is almost zero! Nobody wants it, because of the location, and that's not something you can do anything about. Probably the only thing you can do with such a dog is to rent it out to some marginal tenants.

4. *The house has a serious design flaw.* Maybe the house has only one bedroom. Or perhaps the kitchen is just plain ugly. Or maybe there's only a one-car garage. Or—you get the idea. Somebody goofed. Now nobody wants it.

However, unlike the bad location, the design flaw can often be fixed. You may be able to add more bedrooms, redesign the kitchen, or add another garage. In short, it could be a bargain *if* you have a way of correcting the flaw.

Just be sure that you identify the reason a house is being sold at auction before you bid. If you don't, you could end up either paying too much or buying something that you will have great trouble reselling.

Negotiations

Auction negotiations take place in two different ways. First, there are the negotiations between you and the seller over the terms of the sale. (Do you agree to everything the seller wants in the sales contract?) Second is the actual auction process itself.

The Terms of the Sale

Most auctions I've been to offer terrible terms to the buyer. When you put up your earnest-money check (before the auction is held), you may be asked to agree to the terms and conditions of sale. (Be sure you read them thoroughly and have an attorney or competent and experienced agent help you.) Once you agree, you're locked in. So how do you negotiate?

You can, of course, try to get the terms of the sale changed by the auctioneers. However, my own experience is that they simply aren't interested, before the sale.

Another strategy is *not* to bid at all at the sale. Rather, simply come and observe. Unless the prices are super low and out of this world or the properties are super hot, there are usually a few that don't get sold. In addition, of those that do get sold, more than a few will likely fall through because the buyers ultimately don't qualify for the new mortgage.

After the auction, speak to the selling company. Explain that you're interested in purchasing one of the homes, have the cash, and will get a new mortgage. Offer to negotiate over one of the houses that didn't sell. Or ask the company to call you if one of the "sales" falls through.

Chances are that if the auction company doesn't deal with you immediately, it will call you shortly. Now you can negotiate. No longer does the seller have leverage. The auction is over and it costs thousands of dollars to hold another. The auction company is anxious to sell because a house sitting there is costing someone interest on an existing mortgage. Therefore, you should be able to work out an arrangement that's suitable to both sides.

Bidding at Auction

Let's say that you don't find the terms of the auction agreement onerous. You sign on and are ready to bid.

Now negotiations take the form of bidding strategy. How do you keep the bidding down and get the property you want at a reasonable price?

I do the following. To begin with, I'm never the first to bid on a property that I want. I wait. Perhaps no one else wants the property. If that's the case, just before the auctioneer lets it go, I enter my low bid. If I'm lucky, I've won and that's it.

More than likely, however, others will bid or once I start someone else will chime in. Now it's a matter of trying to ace out the competition.

When more than one person is bidding, it's important to seem like a strong bidder, rather than a reluctant one. The other person bids a price, you immediately come back. You make it clear that you're going to get this property no matter what. (No, of course you're not. But you want to appear that way.)

Another technique is the jump bid. The bids have been moving up at $1000 apiece. Suddenly you jump the bidding by offering $5000 more. As long as it's still below your previously determined maximum acquisition price, you're okay. And the sudden increase may jolt the other buyers into reconsidering. Maybe they'll shy away from you. Maybe you've pushed it over their maximums. A jump bid will often take the steam right out of an auction.

Problems with Auctions

It's important to be aware that sometimes, perhaps rarely, the auctioneer will not be wholly up-front about the auction. Auctioneers are well aware that many more buyers will show up at an absolute auction than at a reserve auction. Consequently, an auction may be advertised as absolute when it isn't quite that way.

For example, I've been to auctions that are supposed to be absolute, yet when the bidding is very low, there always seem to be a couple of people (usually the same ones) in the audience who bid the prices higher. As a result, no properties go for really low prices.

Are these legitimate buyers? I hope so. But it's possible that the auctioneer is using "shills" in the audience to artificially keep prices up. That's illegal in most states. The trouble is, however, that it's very hard to prove that someone is acting in this way.

If you're at an auction and notice that a couple of people bid up only when prices are low, you might suspect that some sort of hanky-panky is afoot. If it were me, I would simply pick up and get out of there. You won't get a good deal at an unfair auction no matter what you do.

Just remember that the vast majority of auctions are run by reputable companies, and you do get what you pay for.

Get Help

As I've repeatedly said, unless you're very knowledgeable about real estate, you can be at the mercy of what the auctioneer says. It's better to spend a few bucks and get the help of a competent real estate attorney than try to do it all for yourself. This is particularly the case when it comes time to sign anything—from the purchase deposit document to the auction agreement. Have it all checked out before you sign. You'll be doing yourself a huge favor.

Index

About the Author

Robert Irwin has been a successful real estate broker for more than 25 years and has helped buyers and sellers alike through every kind of real estate transaction imaginable. He has served as a consultant to lenders, investors, and other brokers and is one of the most knowledgeable and prolific writers in the field. His books include: *Tips & Traps When Buying a Home; Tips & Traps When Selling a Home; Tips & Traps When Mortgage Hunting; Tips & Traps for Saving on All Your Real Estate Taxes; Buy, Rent, & Hold; How to Find Hidden Real Estate Bargains;* and *The McGraw-Hill Real Estate Handbook.*